Chocolate Lover's

COOKBOOK

Shar Levine & Vicki Scudamore

Sterling Publishing Co., Inc.
New York

I'd like to dedicate this book to my best friend and sister, Vicki Scudamore. Vicki, you're always there when I need you and you bring great joy and chocolate into my life. Thanks.

—S.L.

To Shar, whose brilliant wit and creativity never cease to amaze me. I feel lucky to have you as a best friend. To my husband, Charles, who brings lots of sweetness (including chocolate) into my life—thanks for your love and support. To my sons, Brian and Trevor, who always make me proud. Thanks to my parents, Kenneth Lorber and Florence Lorber-Parecki, who taught me the most important values in life, including a love of fine dining.

—V.S.

Photography by Jeff Connery/Printed Light Photography
Illustrations by John Barrigar
Food Stylist: Ann Merling
Additional photo credits on page 95
Designed by Judy Morgan

Library of Congress Cataloging-in-Publication Data

Levine, Shar, 1953–
    Chocolate lover's cookbook / Shar Levine & Vicki Scudamore.
        p.   cm.
    Includes index.
    ISBN 0-8069-4825-6
    1. Cookery (Chocolate)   2. Chocolate.   I. Scudamore, Vicki.
II. Title.
TX767.C5L46   1997
641.6'374—dc20   96-46686
                                                                              CIP

10   9   8   7   6   5   4   3   2   1

Published by Sterling Publishing Company, Inc.
387 Park Avenue South, New York, N.Y. 10016
© 1997 by Shar Levine and Vicki Scudamore
Distributed in Canada by Sterling Publishing
% Canadian Manda Group, One Atlantic Avenue, Suite 105
Toronto, Ontario, Canada M6K 3E7
Distributed in Great Britain and Europe by Cassell PLC
Wellington House, 125 Strand, London WC2R 0BB, England
Distributed in Australia by Capricorn Link (Australia) Pty Ltd.
P.O. Box 6651, Baulkham Hills, Business Centre, NSW 2153, Australia
Printed in Hong Kong
All rights reserved

Sterling ISBN 0-8069-4825-6

CONTENTS

RECIPES

PREFACE

People all over the world love chocolate. They don't save chocolate for special occasions. In Italy, they use a chocolate–nut spread on toast in the morning. In Norway, mothers use thin sheets of chocolate between pieces of bread and send their children to school with chocolate sandwiches. And in Mexico, a chocolate sauce is served on chicken for dinner. Chocolate can be part of every meal!

Using this book, you can create your own chocolate masterpieces. Surprise your friends and family with homemade hand-dipped chocolates, chocolate sculptures, and even chocolate drinks. Learn the history of this treat and discover some science facts. Certain recipes are designed for the young cook in your household; however, when children are working in the kitchen, they will need an adult's supervision.

We know you will love making and eating the recipes in this book. Each of the creations has been taste-tested by our children. Have fun and don't worry—mistakes can always be eaten.

THE CHOCOLATE TREE

Ask a child where chocolate comes from. If the answer was "It grows on trees," that would be correct! There is no such thing as a milk chocolate tree or a white chocolate tree. All chocolate comes from beans that grow on the *Theobroma cacao* tree. This name, given to it by the Swedish naturalist Carl Linnaeus, really suits the tree as *Theobroma* means "food for the gods." Many people confuse the coconut palm, the coca shrub, and the cocoa tree, but these plants are very different and, in fact, are not even related.

The first cocoa trees (or cacao trees) grew wild somewhere in what is now Mexico or northern South America, and later were cultivated by Indians in the area. Today, these trees can grow up to 40 feet tall (about 12 meters), but they are usually trimmed down to about 25 feet (8 meters) to make it easier for people to pick the beans. Cocoa trees grow only in tropical places such as Brazil, Nigeria, Ghana, the Caribbean, and the Philippines.

A cacao or cocoa tree.

The cocoa tree has leaves that can be up to a foot (30 cm) long. After the tree blossoms, green podlike fruit develop on the tree. These football-shaped pods grow to be about ¼ pound (0.1 kilogram). If you cut one of these pods open, you will see it has 5 ribs or divisions. Each division contains between 5 and 10 seeds or beans, as well as pulp. Each tree will grow 20 to 40 pods per year. As only the bean is used, by the time the pod is cut up and the cocoa beans removed, you end up with only 1 to 2 pounds (½ or 1 kilogram) per tree. When the fruit is ripe, the pods are cut off the tree and cut open. The beans and pulp are taken out. The beans and pulp are then fermented by being left in a very warm, closed space for several days. The mixture must be stirred in the containers to give the beans an even flavor. The beans change color and get plumper from the moisture in the containers. When the beans are removed from the containers, they have a rich smell. This fermentation is crucial to developing the chocolate's flavor. The beans and the pulp are then separated, and the beans are washed, dried in special machines, and then put into bags for shipping.

Like coffee beans, cocoa beans must also be roasted before they are used, and like coffee, cocoa beans from different parts of the world are combined to give a desired flavor of chocolate. The roasting gives the bean its flavor, color, and special smell and also makes it easier to break the beans apart. Cocoa nibs, the "meat" of the cocoa beans, are broken up when the beans are cracked by a machine. The shells are winnowed away. The nibs are ground, which generates enough heat to melt the cocoa butter in the beans and results in the thick dark-brown paste called the chocolate liquor. This liquor is not an alcoholic drink, but rather the liquid that is formed by the ground-up beans. The liquor is at least half cocoa butter, which is a vegetable fat. It hardens as it cools. Plain chocolate liquor is molded into blocks or cakes and shipped to chocolate factories to be blended and made into the different kinds of chocolate.

Cocoa beans come in different varieties, depending on where they are grown and what kind of cocoa tree they were grown on. Chocolatiers can tell the difference among these varieties and compare this process to fine wine tasting.

Cross-sections of cacao pods, showing beans.

Cocoa butter at Foley's chocolate factory.

Chocolate panning machine, Foley's chocolate factory.

There is also a variety of mint plant called a chocolate mint. While it does not taste like chocolate, the leaves smell like chocolate when crushed between your fingers.

WHY DOES SOME CHOCOLATE MELT IN YOUR MOUTH?

In 1879, a Swiss chocolatier named Rodolphe Lindt invented a process called *conching*. Vats of chocolate are heated and agitated in a large machine, which helps the chocolate develop its flavor and also smooths out the rough edges of the sugar particles, making the final product smoother and softer. The original troughs looked like seashells, so the inventor called it conching, as *concha* is Spanish for "shell."

CAN I GROW A CHOCOLATE TREE?

Yes and no. Cocoa trees only grow in certain places. Grab an atlas and find the latitude of the place you live in. If it is within 20° north or south of the equator, if it rains at least 50 inches (130 cm) a year, if it stays between about 65°F (18.3°C) and 80°F (27°C), and if it is 100 feet (35 meters) or more above sea level, then you can probably grow a tree.

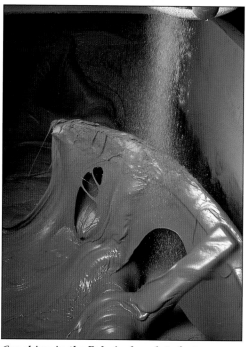

Conching in the Foley's chocolate factory.

THE HISTORY OF CHOCOLATE

THE LEGEND OF CHOCOLATE

The ancient Aztecs and Toltecs, and other tribes in what is now Mexico, believed in a god named Quetzalcoatl, whom they depicted as a feathered serpent. Quetzalcoatl was chief of the wind gods, and was credited with the invention of the useful arts, as well as the calendar. He was said to have taught the people many things, including how to paint, grow corn, create metal objects, and—most important to us—he brought the cocoa tree to the people; previously it had been for the gods alone. The Aztecs said that Quetzalcoatl was tricked by another god into drinking a magic potion, lost all his powers, and was driven out. When Quetzalcoatl returned to the Land of Gold, where the sun rests at night, he promised his people he would come back every 52 years.

Spanish explorer Hernán Cortés arrived in 1519, a year that was one in which Quet-zalcoatl was expected, and the Aztec ruler Montezuma II thought he was Quetzalcoatl! The Aztec ruler greeted the "god" with his favorite drink: cocoa. Cortés had never tasted

The Mayan deity Quetzalcoatl. Drawing based on an ancient carving.

The Mayan glyph for cacao.

An ancient Mayan jar.

A pot containing the residue of cacao dating back to the ancient Mayas was discovered by Dr. Richard Adams in Río Azul, Guatemala, in 1984. Working with computer input from many colleagues, archeologists decoded the Mayan glyphs on the pot, which said it was for holding cacao and belonged to a nobleman. Chemists from Hershey Foods analyzed the pot's contents and proved that the pot, in fact, held 1500-year-old chocolate. Scholars now believe that the hiero-glyphs on jars from this period show that there were different kinds of chocolate used by the Maya.

anything like it before. He saw it built up resistance and helped fight fatigue. He thought cocoa would be something valuable to trade, and so he began to plant cocoa trees wherever he thought they would grow.

Christopher Columbus took back cocoa beans to Spain in 1502, from what is now Nicaragua. No one cared very much, and cocoa didn't catch on until 25 years later, when Cortés returned from the new world. The Spanish kept cocoa for themselves for 100 years, discovering it tasted good when sugar was added. Chocolate was not available to everyone, as it is today. Spanish monks were the only ones allowed to handle the beans. Slowly, word leaked out to other parts of Europe: there was a wonderful new drink.

CHOCOLATE ON THE MOVE

During the Spanish Inquisition, Jews fled Spain for other parts of Europe. They brought the secret of chocolate with them.When Anne of Austria, the daughter of the Spanish king Philip III, married French king Louis XIII in 1615, she took the gift of chocolate to him. The king and his court fell under the spell of this strange liquid. This was a treat that the king felt belonged only to the nobility and tried to keep it away from the common people.

By 1657, a Frenchman opened the first chocolate shop in London, England, selling solid chocolate to be made into drinks. Only the rich could afford to drink it, as the price of a pound of cocoa was high. Chocolate houses began to open all over Europe. Italy, France and England soon discovered the joys of chocolate. In Italy, the Catholic Church thought chocolate to be too rich to be drunk during Lent, until a cardinal, obviously a chocolate lover, declared the drink acceptable.

Chocolate was brought to the United States around the middle of the 1700s. In 1765, a chocolate maker from Ireland, John Hannon, went into business with Dr. James Baker in a grist mill on the Neponset River near Dorchester, Massachusetts. Their company began grinding beans using water power, which made the chocolate smoother than if it were ground by hand. The beans for the chocolate came fresh off the boat from the ships sailing from the West Indies. The business became Baker's Chocolate, but chocolate was still only used as a drink.

In 1828, a Dutch chemist named Conrad van Houten invented the chocolate screw press. This machine squeezed out some of the cocoa butter from the nibs and left the powdery cocoa, which created a less fattening chocolate drink and concentrated the co-

coa butter as a separate ingredient. In 1847, J. S. Fry & Sons in England created the first solid eating chocolate, improving the texture of pure chocolate. He added extra cocoa butter. The first milk chocolate is thought to have been invented by Sir Hans Sloane. It took Swiss chocolatier Daniel Peter to perfect chocolate. He added condensed milk, manufactured by Henri Nestlé, and sugar to the chocolate liquor. Voilà! a new treat was born.

THE SCIENCE OF CHOCOLATE

People throughout the ages have always *loved* chocolate. Chocolate is considered the food of love: a traditional gift for Valentine's Day is a heart-shaped box of chocolates.

Chocolate contains caffeine. The caffeine in coffee makes some people "edgy" or keeps them awake at night. People assume that because chocolate contains caffeine, it will have the same effect; however, a 1½ ounce bar of milk chocolate contains about the same amount of caffeine as a cup of decaffeinated coffee. Chocolate also contains phenylethylamine, or PEA, a compound that is thought to be mood-altering. PEA also is found in the human brain. When something good happens to you, your PEA level increases. This may cause the feelings that people report when they are in love. The cocoa bean contains another stimulant, theobromine, used in making certain medicines.

The cocoa butter in chocolate is a saturated vegetable fat, unlike regular butter. Cocoa butter is used in cosmetics; in particular, in suntan lotions and creams. How fattening is chocolate? A one-ounce (28 g) milk chocolate bar has about 170 calories, about the same number of calories as 8 ounces (224 g) of yogurt, or 2 ounces (56 g) of raisins, or one ounce (28 g) of peanuts. Chocolate contains calcium, protein, potassium, and riboflavin, a B vitamin. The bottom line is: If you don't eat too much chocolate in a day, it won't affect

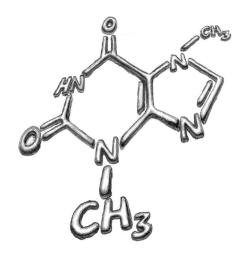

A theobromine molecule.

your weight too much. Pimples are not caused by eating chocolate. Recently, researchers tested teenagers who ate chocolate and those who didn't, to see the effect of chocolate-eating on acne. They discovered that the chocolate in a teen's diet had no effect on skin blemishes.

Don't feel guilty about loving chocolate. The Aztecs believed that chocolate was an aphrodisiac, a stimulant, and was generally good for you!

Various kinds of chocolate.

Molded milk chocolates.

in other countries. Check the definitions in your country for more information.)

Note: Generally, the more expensive a block of chocolate is, the better the quality of chocolate. If you are using very expensive chocolate in your candy-making or baking, you will need less shortening, because of the high percentage of cocoa butter in such chocolates. We only used pure chocolate in our molds, coatings, and candies. Read the label carefully to make sure the chocolate you are using is really chocolate and doesn't contain any milk solids or sweeteners or other ingredients. If it isn't pure chocolate, it may not work for the recipes in this book. Don't substitute chocolate morsels or chips if the recipe calls for solid chocolate. If the recipe calls for semisweet, unsweeted, or milk chocolate, don't use cocoa or chocolate morsels instead.

You probably think there are only two kinds of chocolate: white and dark. Wrong! There are many types of chocolate. The type of chocolate you use in cooking will make a difference to the look and taste of your creation. To be real chocolate, a product must contain chocolate liquor, the liquid made from grinding cocoa beans. In the United States, the federal Food and Drug Administration's Standards of Identity define various percentages of ingredients for each kind of chocolate. (These percentages are different

Chocolate batch blending.

UNSWEETENED CHOCOLATE

Unsweetened chocolate is made of pure chocolate liquor and has no sugar or milk solids added, which means the chocolate may taste bitter. It is used for baking or candy-making, and not for eating in its present state. It is also called *baking chocolate*.

UNSWEETENED COCOA POWDER

Chocolate liquor is pressed, reducing the cocoa butter to 24% or less. This leaves a liquor, which is hardened into press cakes, which are then ground up to create cocoa powder. Cocoa powder is used for baking or for making drinks. Unsweetened cocoa powder is not the same as the chocolate drink mixes you see at the market. Unsweetened cocoa powder is dark brown; the mix is lighter, because the sugar and milk solids in the chocolate drink mix change the color and make the powder sweeter. There may be other ingredients in the mix also. The blacker, denser unsweetened cocoa is called Dutch cocoa. It is generally preferred by bakers because it has been treated with an alkali to make it less bitter and improve its color and flavor in a process called *dutching,* invented by Dutch chemist Conrad van Houten. Unsweetened cocoa should not be confused with sweet cocoa, which may contain as little as 6.8% or

Light, medium and dark chocolate.

more nonfat cocoa solids, and may also have milk solids, bulking agents, and other ingredients. Throughout this book *cocoa* means unsweetened cocoa, unless otherwise noted.

SWEETENED BULK CHOCOLATES

Chocolate liquor is combined with additional cocoa butter, sugar, milk products, flavorings, and emulsifiers, to make sweetened bulk chocolates which are used to produce chocolate for eating or coating chocolate. Sweetened bulk chocolates are available in slabs, wheels, chunks, or wafers. Flavorings may include vanilla, essential oils of lemon, orange, etc. Emulsifiers, such as lecithin, are surface-active agents that permit mixing of fat and other ingredients; they reduce the viscosity of chocolate, thinning it, and reduce the amount of cocoa butter needed. Milk solids and milk fats are used for flavoring milk chocolate and sometimes semisweet chocolate.

Milk Chocolate

According to the United States Standards of Identity, milk chocolate contains not less than 10% by weight of chocolate liquor, not less than 3.39% milkfat, and not less than 12% total milk solids from various dairy ingredients, as well as sugar and flavorings. It is sweetened heavily and may be harder to work with than semisweet chocolate because

of the milk solids in it. Milk chocolate is lighter in color than semisweet or dark chocolate because it has other ingredients added to it. Ounce for ounce, milk chocolate has the most calories of all the kinds of chocolate.

Sweet Chocolate

Sweet chocolate is prepared by mixing and grinding chocolate liquor with sweeteners. It may also contain cocoa butter, spices, cream, milk, or other dairy products, emulsifying agents, and other ingredients. It is ideal for molding, dipping, and spreading, as well as baking and, of course, eating. Sweet chocolate must contain not less than 15% chocolate liquor by weight, and less than 12% by weight of total milk solids according to the standards of identity. Semisweet and bittersweet chocolate are kinds of sweet chocolate that contain not less than 35% chocolate liquor. Unlike unsweetened chocolate, semisweet chocolate is tasty. The chocolate flavor will be stronger if there is more chocolate and less sugar in the bar. Stores sell different grades or types of semisweet chocolate.

White Chocolate

Technically, white chocolate is not really chocolate; at present in the United States it is called *white cocoa butter coating,* because it does not contain any chocolate liquor. White chocolate has cocoa butter in it, which gives it a chocolate flavor, and extra milk products, replacing the absent liquor. Unless the recipe calls for white chocolate, don't use it instead of regular chocolate, because it is sweeter and doesn't bake the same way as dark chocolate. In candy-making, white chocolate can be harder to work with than regular chocolate or milk chocolate. Many white chocolates have a yellow tinge to them. This is the natural color of the cocoa butter in them. White chocolate should not be confused with confectioner's coatings; the latter don't contain cocoa butter (see below.)

Chocolate Chips or Morsels

Chips or morsels are used for making cookies. They may be made with additives or simply use a heavy liquor chocolate with almost no cocoa butter in it to help the chips keep their shape. If you are using these to bake, you will find they don't melt easily and are too thick to use for some recipes, because they contain very little cocoa butter. If you hunt around, you can sometimes find chocolate "buttons," although they are not common. These buttons, larger and flatter than chocolate chips, can be used in most recipes.

Assorted chocolate chips.

CONFECTIONER'S COATINGS

These chocolate-flavored coatings, also called compound coatings or pastel coatings, are not really chocolate, because they substitute other vegetable fats, such as palm kernel oil or coconut oil, for cocoa butter. They can be used for decorating or molding and don't require tempering.

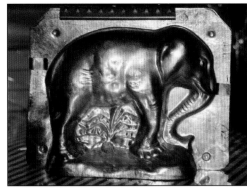
100-year old English chocolate mold.

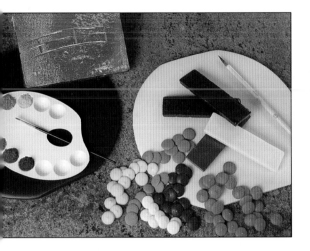

Assorted chocolate-flavored chips.

TERMINALLY TRENDY CHOCOLATE

If you are searching for something unusual in chocolate, try the Internet. Using www.Web Crawler or any other such search program, you can find just about anything you want. Sites include companies from which you can order chocolate supplies and products, recipes, and even chocolate chat lines.

LIQUID CENTERS, BARS, AND HAND-DIPPED CHOCOLATES

Have you ever asked yourself how these chocolates are made? There several methods of creating a liquid-filled chocolate.

LIQUID CENTERS

Shell Method for Bars and Bonbons

A hollow bottom chocolate shell is first made. This shell is then filled with the center. A ⅛-inch (.5 cm) space is left between the filling and the top of the shell. Filling and shell are allowed to set or harden. Liquid chocolate is poured or floated on top, and also hardened.

One-Shot Method

A special machine is used to create a liquid-center chocolate. This machine has a pipe within a pipe and looks like a circle inside a circle. The outside circle or pipe shoots chocolate into a mold. A fraction of a second later, the inside pipe shoots a blob of liquid into the center of the same mold. Meanwhile, the outside pipe continues to inject chocolate into the mold, so the liquid is now enclosed in a chocolate shell.

Dough Method

The chocolate surrounds a doughlike cream filling that is mixed with an enzyme called invertase. In about 10 days, this enzyme breaks down the sugary center into a liquid or creamy filling. Sometimes when you bite into a chocolate-covered cherry which has a clear, liquid center, you can see a solid white sugary casing. This is probably part of the original "dough."

SOLID CHOCOLATE BARS

Chocolate bars have patterns or shapes on their surface. The pattern is engraved into the bottom of the mold. Chocolate is supplied to fill the molds from tempering machines. The chocolate is pumped or bucketed into melters, where nuts, puffed rice, or extra cocoa butter can be added to give the desired texture. The mixture is then poured into the molds. A vibrating machine shakes them to get rid of air bubbles. After cooling on a conveyor belt, the bars are wrapped, boxed, and shipped.

HAND-DIPPED CHOCOLATES

Special centers are made using butters, creams, flavorings, sugars and other things. These are either cooked and cooled or are mixed together without cooking, and may be refrigerated until they are hard or solid enough to work with. Liquid chocolate is then tempered. The centers are rolled by hand in chocolate and placed on wax paper to set.

TOOLS AND SUPPLIES

Now it's time to learn how to make some chocolates ourselves. You will need the following tools in addition to your usual cooking equipment. Special equipment for particular recipes are included in those recipes' materials lists.

➤ Chocolate molds: Special molds available from cookware shops, specialty stores, and chocolate suppliers. Plastic molds are the easiest ones to work with. (See the molding section for more details.)
➤ Tempering spatula, dough scraper, or candy scraper
➤ Wooden spoon, for stirring chocolate
➤ Mat: Something on which you can spread out the chocolate and work it. A marble or granite slab, a plastic mat specially made for this purpose, or a cookie sheet will do. (For our purposes, we will refer to it as a mat.)
➤ Sharp knife or cleaver for cutting block chocolate
➤ Lollipop (sucker) sticks for molds
➤ Paintbrushes: used for decorating. Choose a soft nylon or other paintbrush that doesn't lose its bristles. Candy-making suppliers have special brushes for this purpose
➤ Pastry brush for spreading chocolate
➤ Mallet or rolling pin for breaking up chocolate
➤ Electric warming tray for keeping melted chocolate warm (useful but not essential)
➤ Double boiler or two nesting saucepans, or bowl in a roasting pan for melting chocolate
➤ Thermometer that measures low temperatures, 80°F to 120°F (27°C to 49°C)
➤ Food coloring: Powdered food coloring is best, because liquid food coloring spoils the texture of the chocolate

➤ Shortening: We recommend butter, but you can use vegetable shortening such as margarine
➤ Chocolate: see individual recipes for details

Melted chocolate in the top of a double boiler, a cleaver for cutting chocolate, and block chocolate on a cutting board.

JUNIOR CHOCOLATE MAKERS

Children will need an adult's supervision when using any kitchen appliance involving heat, such as the stove or microwave. If they have any allergies to any of the ingredients, do not use them. Children should check with an adult before trying any of the recipes.

It is important that children wash their hands before working with chocolate. Be sure the kitchen counters and tables on which they are working are clean and clear of unnecessary items before they place any chocolate ingredients on them.

Warning: Melted chocolate can burn you if you are not careful. Adults should assist children by pouring the liquid chocolate onto the tempering surface. Use the spatula to temper or stir the melted chocolate. To avoid burning fingers and tongues, children should not touch or taste the melted chocolate until it has cooled.

INGREDIENTS AND EQUIVALENTS

You can start out with the baking chocolates purchased at the grocer's. Later you may want to purchase chocolate in block form. You can buy really fine chocolate at many chocolate or candy stores, cake decorating supply shops, and gourmet supply shops. The best ingredients are very expensive. If possible, use a good quality block of chocolate, as this will give you the best results.

We prefer butter as our shortening. Some expensive chocolates may require no additional shortening, because the chocolate has a large amount of cocoa butter in it already. As a general rule, we use expensive chocolate when dipping, molding, or decorating. In most other recipes, we use a less expensive chocolate with shortening.

The more cocoa butter the chocolate contains, the thinner (less viscous). Some chocolate chips will not give you the same results in recipes as pure chocolate will, so please try to follow the recipes as given, with as few changes as possible. Below are some useful equivalents.

➤ To make unsweetened chocolate as sweet as semisweet chocolate, add 40% sugar, or about 2½ teaspoons (12.5 mL) per ounce. Stir in the sugar after the chocolate is melted, but before tempering
➤ 1 ounce of chocolate = 4 tablespoons grated chocolate
➤ In an emergency only, 3 tablespoons (45 mL) of cocoa powder may be combined with

1 teaspoon (5 mL) of butter to substitute for a 1-ounce (28 g) square of unsweetened chocolate. Do not use this for making candy or coating desserts
➤ 1 teaspoon (tsp) = 5 mL
➤ 1 tablespoon (T) = 15 mL
➤ 1 cup (U.S. liquid measure) = 8 fluid ounces = 250 mL
➤ 1 pound (455 g) of cocoa = 4 cups
➤ 1 pound (455 g) of butter = 2 cups
➤ 4 ounces (114 g) of butter = 8 tablespoons or ½ cup

STORAGE

1. Keep chocolate supplies wrapped up in a cool place (65° to 70°F or 18° to 21°C), away from things that have a strong smell. Chocolate can pick up the odors of other foods, which may ruin the tempting chocolate fragrance. Do not leave your chocolate in the refrigerator or freezer (unless indicated in a recipe to do so).

2. If your chocolate has a gray or whitish color, it doesn't mean it has gone bad. Chocolate will "bloom" or turn white when it has been left someplace warm, as the cocoa butter rises to the surface. Tempering it will restore its color.

MELTING AND TEMPERING

In order to use chocolate for candy-making or dipping, it must be *tempered*. The liquid cocoa butter in melted chocolate is a mixture of fat that can recrystallize either in stable or in unstable forms when it cools. In its stable form it will be glossy, firm chocolate. If unstable, it will be slow to set, granular, and dull-looking, with patches of gray bloom. Tempering is the method of getting the cocoa butter in the fluid chocolate into stable crystalline form. Two basic methods of tempering chocolate are given below. The first stage is melting the chocolate; then it must be cooled and tempered. Once you get used to this process, you will be able to sense the correct temperatures by hand. Use a thermometer that covers the low range, 70° to 130°F (21.1° to 54.4°C) while you are learning, until you feel comfortable without it. Chocolate must be tempered again each time it is melted.

Tempering Method 1

1. Divide the chocolate into small pieces, by cutting, hitting it with a mallet or rolling pin, or grating it. It melts much more quickly when it is chopped up.

2. Melt the chocolate slowly over water that is not more than 120°F (49°C). Heat water on the stove in the bottom of a double boiler to 120°F (49°C) and remove it from the stove. Fill the top part of the double boiler with part of the chopped-up chocolate and set it in the bottom part.

3. As it melts, begin to stir the chocolate. Once it is almost all melted, continue to stir. Let the chocolate warm until it is between 110°F (43.3°C) and 120°F (49°C), as measured by a dry thermometer.

4. Replace the 120°F water below the chocolate with 95°F (35°C) water and set the melted chocolate back over it. Cool the chocolate, stirring occasionally, until it reaches 90°F–95°F (32.2°C–35°C).

5. If the recipe calls for shortening, add shortening to the melted chocolate. Stir to mix it completely.

6. Wipe off the bottom of the pot. Pour about half of the melted chocolate onto your marble slab or mat. Spread it across the mat's surface with a spatula, candy scraper or other tool and work it back and forth until it becomes pastelike, takes on a matte appearance, and is 80°F (26.7°C). Don't let it get below 77°F (25°C). Keep the rest of the chocolate warm at 90° to 95°F (32.2° to 35°C).

7. Scrape up the chocolate on the slab and put it in a bowl. Warm the chocolate from the slab up to 86° to 90°F (30° to 32.2°C) for dark chocolate or 83° to 88°F (28.3° to 31°C) for milk or white chocolate by gradually adding the 90°–95°F reserved chocolate. Stir well.

8. To test the tempering, place a drop of tempered chocolate on a piece of wax paper in the refrigerator for about 3 minutes. It should become smooth and shiny. If it is still soft and tacky at that time, it probably isn't in temper. If so, reheat to 120°F (49°C) and repeat the process. If it is in temper, you can use it for molding or whatever purpose you need.

Left: Chocolate that has seized. Right: tempered chocolate.

Tempering Method 2

Method 2 is for use with chocolate that is already in temper when you buy it.

1. Make shavings of about 10% of your chocolate block, using a very fine cheese grater. Set the shavings aside.

2. Chop up and melt the remaining 90% of your chocolate in the top of a double boiler over hot water (120°F, 49°C) until the chocolate is 110°F (43.3°C).

3. Replace the water in the outer pot with water at 70°F (21°C) and cool the chocolate down to 90°F (32.2°C). Stir slowly and constantly. At 93°F (34°C) stir and mix in the chocolate shavings.

4. Maintain a temperature of 90°F (32.2°C) for dark chocolate and 87°F (30.5°C) for milk or white chocolate. Use it for coating or pouring your molds.

5. Place the chocolates in a room cooler than 70°F (21°C) to cool. Do not refrigerate.

Working with chocolate is a skill, and like any other skill, it takes time and practice to develop.

MORE ABOUT MELTING AND TEMPERING

1. Never melt chocolate with a lid on the pot. Steam will collect on the inside of the lid and water will drip down into your chocolate. Even a tiny drop of water will cause it to "seize" and "tighten" (harden or stiffen). If you get any water in your melted chocolate, add ½ teaspoon or more of vegetable oil to the melted mixture. This might save your mixture.

2. White chocolate is harder to work with than dark or milk chocolate. Be sure not to heat it over 120°F (49°C) or you will scorch the milk. For your final handling temperature try to keep it 1° or 2° cooler than you would with milk chocolate.

3. For dipping chocolates, the temperature should be between 86°F and 89°F (30° and 31.6°C) for milk chocolate and 89° and 91°F (31.7° and 32.8°C) for semisweet.

4. Chocolate can be melted in a microwave. This works best for a cup or two of chocolate, not more. Grate the chocolate and place it in a microwavable dish. Do not cover. Microwave semisweet on medium heat and white and milk chocolate on low heat. Microwave for 20 seconds and stir. Keep doing this until the chocolate is just about melted. Adjust the timing based on the results in your particular microwave. Check the temperature of the chocolate with a thermometer. It should be about 110°–125°F (43.3°–51.7°C). Proceed as above for tempering.

COOLING AND STORING FINISHED WORK

After you have molded, dipped, or otherwise made chocolate candies, cool them as follows.

Some recipes call for chocolate curls for decoration. Make these by scraping a sharp knife along the top of a block of chocolate.

1. Put the chocolates on a cooling rack in a cool room (50° to 55°F or 10° to 12.8°C), or chill them in the refrigerator until set.

2. Let them warm to 65° to 70°F (18.3° to 21.1°C).

3. Store them for at least 24 hours, uncovered, at the same temperature before wrapping them, to be sure they are cool throughout.

Chocolate before and after being microwaved. Whisk is used to mix or stir the chocolate.

RECIPES

MOLDED CHOCOLATES

Have you ever wondered how chocolate Easter bunnies and chocolate Santas get their shapes? In the factory, tempered chocolate is poured into molds. It then goes on a bumpy ride down a conveyor belt to shake out the air bubbles. After the roller-coaster ride comes the cooling tunnel, where the liquid chocolate becomes solid. Chocolate bars are made in flat molds. Chocolates with designs on both sides, like Easter bunnies, are made with a double mold; they may be solid or hollow. If you look carefully at a bunny, you can see seams along the sides where the halves were joined.

GENERAL MOLDING INSTRUCTIONS

Purchase plastic molds specially made for chocolate in the shapes you like. (There are also metal molds, but they are a bit harder to use.) You can get free molds by using the plastic container that holds an Easter bunny or egg. Chocolate advent calendars make great molds. Wash them in warm, soapy water before the first use. Be careful not to use any cleaners on them that may scratch them. Do not put them in the dishwasher. Do not oil the molds; chocolate, if properly tempered, will pop out of them when it is set. Molding is done with melted and tempered chocolate, so melt and temper the chocolate as described in the general instructions. Our recipes include shortening, but if you are working with expensive chocolate, you probably won't need to add shortening, because the chocolate itself will have a high amount of cocoa butter in it. There are basically two kinds of molds: flat and hollow.

Flat molds (one-sided molds). Flat molds are sheets of plastic or metal with a depres-

Unmolding a bunny at Charlie's Chocolate Factory, Vancouver, B.C.

sion containing some sort of design on the front in low relief. (In some cases there is a matching back given also, which lets you mold both parts and stick them together with liquid chocolate to make a flat chocolate with a design on both sides). Lollypop (sucker) molds are flat molds that have an additional depression in which you can put a lollypop stick after the chocolate is poured into the mold.

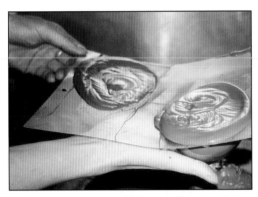

Filling a two-part mold for a solid chocolate.

To use flat molds, spoon the tempered chocolate into each depression, but do not fill them to overflowing or the backs will need trimming. Rap them on the counter to release any air bubbles, and then let them cool until they are set in a cool room or the refrigerator (don't leave uncovered chocolates in the refrigerator too long or they will absorb excess moisture, however). To unmold, turn the mold upside down over a counter and flex the mold a bit.

Hollow molds have two sides, and are usually more sculptural than flat molds. Some come with pins to hold them together; others must be clamped together with paper clamps. Hollow molds can be used to make solid shapes, hollow shapes, or filled chocolates.

Hollow shapes from two-sided molds. To mold hollow shapes, spoon or funnel tempered chocolate into one-half of the hollow mold. Rap the filled mold on the work counter to shake out any air bubbles. Clamp the unfilled half of the mold in place on all sides, lining up the edges carefully. Rotate the mold several times to coat the inside of the unfilled half with chocolate. Let cool with the newly filled side down for a few minutes; then reverse the position; repeat this turning until the piece seems firm. Then release the lips and let the piece cool until completely set. Remove one side of the mold first, then the other, when unmolding.

Solid shapes from two-sided molds. To mold solid shapes, fill both sides of a hollow mold with tempered chocolate, but fill one side less full than the other. Have your clamps nearby if the mold doesn't have its own locks. Grasp one side of the filled mold with each hand, and flip one-half over the other, being sure the sides are well aligned. Squeeze the pieces together and clamp them. Let the mold cool bottom-side up.

Cooling and unmolding. You will learn from experience how long to let the mold cool. When the surface of the chocolate looks frosted throughout when you look through the plastic, that is a sign that it is ready to be unmolded. Let the molds cool in a cool room or in the refrigerator until the chocolate is set and hard. The time varies depending on the thickness of the piece molded. Gently push the chocolates from the mold to remove them when the chocolate is set. Trim the excess from the bottom or seams of the mold with a knife so the outlines are clear and smooth. Clean the molds by rinsing in warm water and dry carefully. Store the molds flat so they don't warp.

Chocolate Lollypops (Suckers)

Here is a perfect activity to do with a child. Purchase a special lollypop (sucker) mold and follow the simple instructions given below, after reading the general instructions on melting and tempering chocolate given earlier in the book. *Number of lollypops varies with mold.*

8 oz	semisweet, milk, or white chocolate	227 g
1 tsp	butter	5 mL
	lollypop sticks	

1. Melt the chocolate by the microwave or double-boiler method (see general instructions on melting and tempering chocolate).
2. When the chocolate has melted, add the butter and stir until it is well blended.
3. Pour the chocolate onto the mat and temper it, according to the tempering instructions in the general instructions section.
4. Fill the molds with chocolate, using the spatula or a spoon. Do not grease the molds. Lay a pop stick onto the middle of the soft chocolate; rotate it to be sure it is coated on all sides. Gently tap the mold on the counter to remove air bubbles. Place the molds in the refrigerator or another cool place.
5. Take the molds out of the fridge after about 10 minutes. If you look at the bottom of the mold (the designed side) you can see if the chocolate has pulled away from the inside of the mold, indicating that it is set. Turn the mold upside down on waxed paper, and the pieces should fall out. If not, rap the inverted mold on the counter.
6. Scrape up the leftover chocolate from the mat and remelt it as needed.

Chocolate Baskets

Making a chocolate basket. Lower left, the finished basket, filled with candy.

How would you like to eat the basket your chocolates come in? If you think a wicker basket would taste awful, how about a chocolate basket? *Makes 6 baskets.*

8 oz	semisweet or milk chocolate	227 g
1 tsp	butter or margarine	5 mL
	large size freezer bag or piece of heavy plastic wrap	
6	4 oz (125 mL) cups or soufflé dishes	

1. Cut the plastic bag apart so you have two rectangles or use plastic wrap.

2. Melt chocolate and temper following the general instructions. Put some tempered chocolate onto one piece of plastic, and spread it into a circular shape with a candy scraper.

3. Place the chocolate, plastic side down, over a cup or soufflé dish. Shape it by pulling the plastic down around the sides of the cup. Let the piece cool in a cool room or in the refrigerator.

4. When the chocolate has hardened, remove it from the cup and peel off the plastic. Fill your chocolate basket with fruit or treats.

Chocolate Balloons

Here is a great idea for a birthday party activity. Every child loves balloons and here's one that won't blow away in the wind. *Makes six 10-inch balloons.*

6	10-inch (25 cm) round balloons	
16 oz	semisweet or milk chocolate	455 g
1 T	butter or margarine	15 mL
	large mixing bowl	
	wax-paper-covered cookie sheet	
	pastry brush (optional)	

1. Inflate the balloons. Clean and dry the outside of the balloons, making sure there is no water left on the surface.

2. Melt the chocolate, stir in the shortening, and temper, following the general instructions.

3. Put the tempered chocolate into the mixing bowl.

4. Place the bottom of the balloon in the tempered chocolate and gently rock the balloon back and forth to cover the bottom quarter of the balloon. Do not cover too much of the balloon as the chocolate will crack when the balloon pops. Another method is to place the tied end of a balloon in the mixing bowl and use a pastry brush to paint the chocolate onto the balloon.

5. Place the dipped balloon on the cookie sheet covered with waxed paper, or suspend the balloon from a rack in the refrigerator. Allow the chocolate to thoroughly harden. The balloon will start to shrink and pull away from the sides of the chocolate.

6. Remove from the refrigerator when it is hardened, which may take several hours. Pop the balloon and remove all pieces of the balloon from the chocolate.

7. To serve, fill with treats, fruit, or ice cream.

Chocolate Boxes and Cups

Making chocolate cups.

Making a chocolate box.

If you haven't got any balloons, but you'd still like to eat your containers, here's another project. *Makes 12 boxes or cups.*

8 oz	semisweet chocolate	227 g
1 tsp	butter or margarine	5 mL
24	cupcake liners (for cups) or empty, individual sized cereal boxes	
	spoon or pastry brush	
	cookie sheet covered with waxed paper or aluminum foil	
	plastic food wrap	

1. Melt and temper the chocolate following the melting and tempering instructions in the general instructions section of the book.

FOR CUPS

2. For each cup, place two cupcake liners together, one inside the other. Paint a thick layer of tempered chocolate on the inside of each pair of cups, making sure to cover the top and bottom of the cups with lots of chocolate. Place them on the cookie sheet and leave them in the refrigerator until hardened (about ½ hour).

FOR BOXES

3. Wrap the outside of each box with plastic wrap. Smooth it down to create as few bumps and creases as possible. Paint a layer of melted chocolate on the outside of each box. Do not paint the top of the box, only the bottom and 4 sides. Put extra chocolate on the bottom and the corners. Turn it upside down and place on cookie sheet with waxed paper. Put the boxes in the fridge until hard.

REMOVING THE CHOCOLATE SHELL

4. Carefully peel the paper or plastic away from the chocolate, leaving the shape. If there are any bare spots or cracks, don't worry. Paint chocolate over these spots and let it harden. No one will notice.

Giant Peanut Butter Cups

You can figure out what a chocolate manufacturer might call these delights. We call them giant peanut butter cups. *Makes 12 cups.*

12	chocolate cups*	
2–3 cups	peanut butter	500–750 mL
⅓–½ cup	butter or margarine	75 to 125 g
8 oz	semisweet chocolate	227 g
1 tsp	butter or margarine (for chocolate)	5 mL

See the Chocolate Boxes and Cups recipe to make these.

1. Melt the peanut butter in a double boiler until it is runny. Add the ⅓–½ cup butter in pieces and stir until smooth. Cool to room temperature.

2. Pour the peanut butter mixture into the frozen chocolate cups and place in the fridge to harden.

3. After the cups have hardened, you are ready for the next step. Melt and temper the chocolate as described in the general instructions section of the book; add the teaspoon of butter to the melted chocolate before tempering. Spoon the tempered chocolate over the cups to form a top layer. Return these to the fridge and allow them to set completely.

4. Store in the fridge.

No ice cream would be complete without a chocolate sauce. Here are two of our favorite toppings.

Paul's Hot Fudge Sauce

My husband loves strong coffees. He is famous for claiming he's on a diet, while adding a serious amount of chocolate syrup to the bottom of his coffee cup. This is his idea of a good time. *Makes 2 servings.*

8 oz	dark semisweet chocolate	227 g
¾ cup	evaporated milk	175 mL
½ tsp	vanilla or other flavoring (optional)	2.5 mL

1. Chop the chocolate into pieces and place it in a pot. Add the milk and warm the mixture over low heat, stirring continually, until the chocolate has melted.
2. Remove from heat immediately and stir in flavoring, if desired. Serve warm.

Brian's Chocolate Syrup

This recipe is dedicated to Vicki's son Brian, who used to drink chocolate syrup from the can when he was a child. *Makes 2 cups of syrup.*

6 oz	semisweet chocolate	170 g
1 cup	water	250 mL
1¼ cups	sugar	300 mL
1 tsp	vanilla extract	5 mL
pinch	salt	

1. Chop the chocolate into pieces and place in a medium-sized pot. Add a pinch of salt and ¼ cup (60 mL) of the water and melt the mixture slowly to make a paste. Stir until smooth.

2. Add the remaining sugar and water and stir until it comes to a boil. Turn the heat to low, and boil for 5 minutes.

3. Remove from heat and allow to cool. Stir in vanilla and store the mixture in a bottle in the fridge.

Here are some cool delights for a warm day, a children's party, or an after-dinner treat, including the ultimate frozen treat, ice cream. Even if you don't have an ice cream machine, you can still make a great icy dessert.

Chocolate Ice Cream

I scream. You scream. Well, you know the rest. Make your own chocolate ice cream. All you really need is a mixer. *Makes 8 servings.*

½ cup	unsweetened cocoa powder	125 mL
2 cups	sugar	500 mL
2 cups	whipping cream	500 mL
3 cups	cereal cream (half and half)	750 mL
1 tsp	vanilla extract	5 mL
	ice-cream maker (optional)	

1. Place the cocoa powder, sugar, and whipping cream in a large pot and stir the mixture over medium heat until the sugar dissolves.
2. Remove from heat and place in fridge until cool (about 15 minutes).
3. Take the mixture from the fridge and add vanilla and cereal cream (half and half). Stir or beat until the cream is blended with the cocoa mixture.
4. Freeze in an ice-cream maker, or place the mixture in the freezer for about 2 hours. Remove from the freezer and beat until the mixture is soft, but not too runny. Freeze again. Repeat these steps two more times.

Chocolate Frozen Yogurt

If you want something different and a little tart, how about chocolate frozen yogurt? *Makes 4 servings.*

2 tsp	cornstarch	10 mL
½ cup	sugar	125 mL
2 cups	evaporated milk	500 mL
1	egg	
1 cup	store-bought or homemade chocolate syrup	250 mL
1 tsp	vanilla extract	5 mL
1½ cups	french vanilla yogurt or plain yogurt	375 mL
	ice-cream maker (optional)	

1. Place sugar, cornstarch, milk, and egg in a large pot and mix with a wooden spoon.

2. Cook this mixture over low heat for about 10 minutes, watching it carefully so it does not burn.

3. Remove the pot from the heat and quickly add in the syrup and mix. Place in the fridge and allow to cool (about 15 minutes).

4. Add the yogurt and vanilla and mix by hand or with an electric mixer until they blend.

5. Freeze in the ice-cream maker, or follow the directions in Step 4 of the Chocolate Ice Cream recipe.

CHOCOLATE FOR FUN AND MONEY

Here are a few ways to enjoy your passion for chocolate and do something good at the same time. Chocolate makes a wonderful focus for a fund-raising event. Some ideas you might wish to try include:

➤ Organize a chocolate buffet. Have each person bring a fancy chocolate dessert and charge an admission to the buffet.

➤ Ask local restaurants, bakeries, caterers and celebrities to donate a gourmet chocolate dessert and raffle off the items at a champagne-and-chocolate evening.

➤ Have a chocolate "cake walk" in which each person who enters wins a chocolate goodie.

➤ Ask local chocolatiers to donate a chocolate creation which you can auction or raffle at an event.

Frozen Bananas

Here's a great way to combine fruit and chocolate in a frozen treat. *Makes 6 servings.*

8 oz	chocolate (any kind)	227 g
1 tsp	butter or margarine	5 mL
6	ripe, but not soft bananas	
6	skewers	
	wax-paper-covered cookie sheet	
8 oz	finely chopped nuts or coconut (optional)	227 g

1. Peel the bananas and cut in half crosswise (not lengthwise). Insert a skewer in the cut part of each half of the banana for a stick or handle. Place the bananas in the freezer overnight to harden.

2. Melt and temper the chocolate, adding the teaspoon of butter or margarine to the melted chocolate before tempering, according to the instructions given in the general instructions section.

3. Dip the frozen bananas into the melted chocolate; roll them in finely chopped nuts or coconut, if you wish. Place on the wax-paper-covered cookie sheet.

4. Place the dipped bananas in the freezer and allow them to harden. Wrap the finished bananas in plastic wrap and store in the freezer.

Frozen Caffeine Buzz

There are certain times when you really need a coffee pick-me-up. If you live in the Pacific Northwest, you can usually satisfy your craving by visiting one of the ubiquitous coffeehouses located on nearly every street corner. This is one dessert which is easy to make but difficult to keep around. We find it tends to disappear when left in the freezer, with only a spoon left in the empty container. *Makes 8 servings.*

FOR CHOCOLATE COOKIE BASE

8 oz	butter	227 g
1 cup	sugar	250 mL
1 cup	packed brown sugar	250 mL
2	large eggs	
1 T	vanilla	15 mL
1 tsp	baking soda	5 mL
1 tsp	baking powder	5 mL
3 cups	flour	750 mL
pinch	salt	
12 oz	real chocolate chips or bar chocolate, broken into pieces	340 g
1 cup	chopped pecans	250 mL
	loaf pan (needed for assembling)	

FOR FILLING AND TOPPING

2 quarts	coffee-flavored ice cream, slightly softened	1.9 L
4 oz	chocolate-covered espresso beans (see recipe below)	114 g
2 cups	whipped cream (optional)	500 mL
1 T	instant coffee granules	15 mL

FOR COFFEE BEANS

4 oz	roasted espresso beans	114 g
8 oz	semisweet chocolate	227 g
1 T	butter or margarine	15 mL
	rolling pin	

TO MAKE THE COOKIES

1. Heat an oven to 350°F (177°C).

2. Cream the butter, then add sugars and beat until smooth.

3. Add the eggs and beat for 1 minute.

4. Add the vanilla, baking soda, baking powder, salt, and flour and mix.

5. Add the chocolate and pecans and mix by hand. Scoop this cookie dough into large balls, using a small ice cream scoop or measuring cup.

6. Place the balls on a prepared cookie sheet, flatten them with a spatula, and bake in a 350°F (177°C) oven for 15 minutes or until a toothpick comes out clean when poked into the center of the cookie.

7. Remove the cookies while they are still soft. Cool on wire rack.

CHOCOLATE-COVERED ESPRESSO BEANS

Use the basic recipe of 8 ounces (227 g) chocolate and 1 tablespoon (15 mL) butter or margarine and melt and temper the semisweet chocolate (see the general instructions). Use the round end of a turkey skewer or wooden skewer to dip each freshly roasted dark coffee bean in the cooled chocolate. Try not to coat the bean with too much chocolate as it will overwhelm the flavor of the bean. Leave on waxed paper to set. To crush, place between 2 sheets of wax paper or in a freezer bag and crush with a rolling pin.

Note: Store-bought espresso beans look shiny not only because of the machines used to create the even texture, but also because of a special coating over the finished chocolate product. The only way to achieve a smooth surface at home is to use a plastic mold.

TO ASSEMBLE

1. Place a layer of chocolate chip cookies on the bottom of a long loaf pan.

2. Cover with a 2-inch (5 cm) layer of softened coffee-flavored ice cream.

3. Sprinkle the top of the ice cream with crushed chocolate-covered espresso beans.

4. Place another layer of cookies over the ice cream, then another layer of ice cream.

5. If you wish, top the ice cream off with coffee-flavored whipped cream. To make it, whip the cream and add a tablespoon of instant coffee granules, or a tablespoon of strong coffee for flavoring.

6. Add a sprinkling of the crushed beans to the top and freeze the dessert overnight.

7. Remove from the freezer shortly before serving and cut with a hot knife.

DECORATIONS

Chocolate is not only fun to eat, it is fun to play with. You can design your own chocolate decorations to adorn any of the treats you bake. Children can surprise their moms with a chocolate butterfly or make a chocolate leaf to set on chocolate bark.

Chocolate Leaves

If you go past the window of a fancy bakery, you sometimes see chocolate leaves on cakes. These edible leaves are incredibly easy to make. You need real leaves to make them with: thick-veined, nonpoisonous leaves—for example, lemon, nonprickly rose leaves, grape ivy (not other ivy)—are perfect. If you are not sure the leaf is safe, call a local nursery or even the poison control office in your city and ask which leaves in your area are safe to use for this purpose. *Makes 12 leaves.*

12	leaves	
8 oz	semisweet or white chocolate	227 g
1 tsp	butter or margarine	5 mL
	paintbrush	
	waxed paper	
	powdered green food coloring (optional with white chocolate)	

1. Wash the leaves in soapy water and dry well. Make sure there is no water on the leaves.

2. Melt the chocolate, stir in the shortening, and temper the chocolate, following the general instructions. If you wish to, dye the white chocolate with green food coloring for realistic leaves.

3. Carefully paint the bottom, veiny part of the leaf and place it, chocolate-side up, on waxed paper.

4. Place the painted leaves in the fridge until the chocolate is hard.

5. Starting from the stem, gently peel the leaf off the chocolate.

Butterflies, Hearts, and Letters

Wouldn't you love a chocolate butterfly floating into your mouth? Here's a simple way to make complicated designs from chocolate. This will take some patience, but the result will be worth it!

8 oz	semisweet or white chocolate	227 g
1 tsp	butter or margarine	5 mL
	felt pen	
	piece of paper	
	waxed paper	
	pastry bag with fine tip or decorating tube	

1. Melt the chocolate, add the shortening, and temper the chocolate following the instructions in the general instructions section.

2. Draw a design such as a butterfly, flower, or a letter on a piece of paper. Keep the design simple the first few times, until you get experienced in using the pastry bag or tube.

3. Place the waxed paper over the design.

4. Fill the pastry bag with chocolate and slowly squeeze chocolate onto the wax paper along the design lines.

5. Place the finished designs in the fridge to harden; then peel back the paper to remove the chocolate designs.

Cookie-Cutter Chocolate

Do you have a favorite cookie shape? Here's a way to make shaped chocolate candies rather than sugar cookies. Use your favorite cookie cutters. You can also make chocolate coins by using round cookie cutters.

8 oz	semisweet chocolate	227 g
1 tsp	butter or margarine	5 mL
	waxed paper	
	cookie cutter	
	cookie sheet or tray	

1. Melt the chocolate, add the butter or margarine, and temper the chocolate following the instructions in the general instructions section.

2. Pour the tempered chocolate onto a cookie sheet covered with waxed paper, and smooth it out to an even layer with the spatula.

3. Place it in the fridge for several minutes. Do not leave it in too long, or the chocolate will break when you cut it.

4. Press a cookie cutter into the chocolate, making sure it goes all the way through the chocolate. Do not lift the chocolate shapes; leave them in place.

5. Keep cutting out shapes, as many as will fit. Return the chocolate to the fridge for at least an hour.

6. Peel the chocolate shapes off the waxed paper. The leftover chocolate can be saved and remelted next time.

Doodles

Vicki's son Trevor loves to draw and thinks the best kinds of drawings are ones he can make and then eat. Do you often doodle with a pen while daydreaming? How about making some chocolate doodles?

	Heavyweight, freezer-type, locking plastic sandwich bag	
2 oz	**semisweet or milk chocolate**	56 g
½ tsp	**butter or margarine**	2.5 mL
	scissors	
	wax-paper-covered cookie sheet or tray	

1. Melt the chocolate in a bowl over hot water or by the microwave method; stir in the shortening and temper the chocolate (see general instructions on melting and tempering).

2. Put the tempered chocolate in the plastic bag, and squeeze the chocolate into one corner of the bag.

3. Cut a small hole in the corner of the bag to form the writing end.

4. Squeeze out the chocolate slowly onto the wax paper in the doodle shapes you want.

5. Put the tray of doodles in the fridge to harden until firm; then peel them off the paper. Use them to decorate drinks or other treats.

How would you like to make chocolate paintings and sculptures? Here are some fun activities for children of any age.

Chocolate Paints

6 oz	pure chocolate bar*	170 g
2 oz	colored confectionery morsels (available in specialty candy stores) or white chocolate	56 g
	paintbrush	
	powdered food coloring**	
	tin cups or small muffin tin	
	electric warming tray or pan of warm water	

Do not use one with nuts, raisins or cereal.
**Use powdered food coloring if possible. Liquid food coloring will cause your chocolate to "seize," or turn grainy. If you use liquid food coloring, add a teaspoon of solid vegetable shortening to smooth out the chocolate. Even with shortening, your colored chocolate will not be as smooth or spreadable as the coloring made with powdered food coloring. If you use colored confectionery morsels, you don't need the food coloring.*

1. Melt the white chocolate or colored confectionery morsels over hot water or in 20-second intervals in the microwave; see the general instructions section of the book.

2. Place a portion of the melted white chocolate in a small cup or tin for each color of food coloring you want to use. Add powdered food coloring to each portion and mix it through. Temper each color of the chocolate until it is cool—about 86–89°F (30–32°C)—and the colors are mixed. See general instructions on tempering. (If you use colored confectionery coating morsels, they don't need to be tempered, as they don't have cocoa butter in them.)

3. Place the tins in a pan of warm water or on a warming tray; keep the chocolate or confectionery paints at about 90°F (32.5°C) so they remain liquid enough to work with. Be sure not to get any water in the chocolate.

4. Unwrap the chocolate bar and turn it flat-side up. Wipe the surface of the chocolate with a cloth to remove any chocolate dust and smooth the surface. Dip a paintbrush into the melted chocolate or confectionery morsels and paint pictures or even greetings onto your chocolate canvas.

5. Let the bar cool and rewrap it.

A hand-painted copy of a Monet done in chocolate by the Hearts & Flowers Candy Company, Hicksville, N.Y. Each of their chocolate bars reproduces a painting by a famous artist. Special edible chocolate paints are used, and techniques are similar to those used are for applying oils to canvas.

Painted Party Invitations

Make birthday party invitations or greeting cards with your chocolate paints. This is a perfect gift for Valentine's Day, Mother's Day, or Father's Day! Buy small rectangular chocolate bars and use them as placecards for your next party.

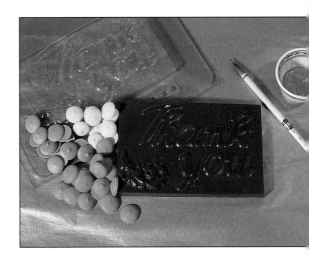

Carved Chocolate Sculpture

Chef David Brown notes: "The unprotected environment of an open lobby in tropical Hawaii poses many problems to the chocolate sculptor. It is necessary to provide an appropriate internal structure to ensure the longevity and safety of the piece. In this case, an iron armature was cemented into a concrete base to supply the counterweight of the top-heavy piece. After this was accomplished, chocolate was added and carved accordingly. After the chocolate was polished with soft towels, it was sprayed with a mixture of one part couverture to one part cocoa butter that was melted to 90°F [32.2°C]."

One of the most remarkable sculptures we have ever seen was not in a museum. It was, in fact, in the foyer of the Hilton Waikoloa Village, on the big island of Hawaii. Executive Pastry Chef David Brown creates life-sized models of angels, birds, and animals. These 7-foot (2.1 m) chocolate works of art are truly masterpieces. The chef won't part with all his secrets, but he was willing to give us some idea of how the sculpture holds together. He also was kind enough to share recipes for several of his most famous dessert creations with us. For those of you who like art projects, here are some hints on how to create an edible sculpture. If you wish to learn more about chocolate carving, David teaches beginning and advanced pastry making at the University of Hawaii at Kealakekua. He is also a past member of the U.S. World Cup Pastry Team and has won various awards and competitions.

FOR CHOCOLATE CARVING

solid block of milk or dark chocolate
craft knife
woodcarving tools
paper and pencil
small craft hammer
cookie sheet

1. Start with a small project, such as a turtle or an alphabet letter. On a piece of paper, mark off the size of one of the sides of your block of chocolate, and draw a simple pattern to fit the size of your block. If possible, try to draw separate sketches showing the shape in three dimensions also, from several views.
2. Cut the pattern out and use the craft knife to trace it onto the appropriate side of the block of chocolate.

3. Using woodcarving tools and a hammer, start cutting away the large areas that need to be removed from the block of chocolate. Carve large shavings off the block of chocolate to create a general shape of the sculpture. *Warning:* When sculpting fine details, carve the chocolate gently. If you hit the chocolate too hard, large pieces will break off.

4. After creating the general form, begin to shape your sculpture using the fine tools, cutting less at a time. If you break off an important part of your sculpture, it is possible to reattach it to the block using melted chocolate; you will see a seam or line, but at least you won't have to start again.

5. Don't try to warm up your tools as it will cause the chocolate to pool and discolor. Don't try to carve small, detailed features or something too deep, as the chocolate will crack.

6. Save all the shavings for use in other chocolate-making recipes.

Plastic Chocolate Centerpiece

Here's a way to make your own centerpieces from chocolate.

6 oz	dark chocolate and	170 g
3 T	white karo syrup	45 mL
	OR	
5 oz	white chocolate and	142 g
2 T	white karo syrup	30 mL
	wooden spoon	
	thick, sealable plastic freezer bag (medium size)	

1. Melt the chocolate over hot water or microwave until the chocolate is all melted; see general instructions for melting information.

2. Warm the karo syrup in a microwave or over hot water so that it is just above room temperature.

3. Stir the karo syrup into the melted chocolate and mix them with a wooden spoon.

4. Pour the mixture into the freezer bag and squeeze the air from the bag. Tightly seal the bag and leave on the kitchen counter overnight.

5. Unseal the edge of the bag and microwave for several seconds on low power, or if you don't have a microwave, warm the sealed bag for a minute or two in warm water, being sure not to get any water in the bag.

6. Squeeze the bag until the mixture is soft; then remove the mixture from the bag and shape the contents into whatever creations you like. Place in the fridge to set.

If you can't make it to the big island to see the chocolate sculptures described in Carved Chocolate Sculpture, you can still enjoy a chocolate dessert from the Hilton Waikoloa Village Hotel. From Chef David Brown, here are 3 luscious creations.

Orange-Ginger Chocolate Sauce

Makes 8 servings.

2 cups	cereal cream (half and half)	500 mL
	zest of 2 oranges	
1 T	chopped fresh ginger	15 mL
¼ cup	sugar	60 mL
1 lb	unsweetened chocolate	455 g
2 oz	unsalted butter	55 g
	strainer	

1. In a heavy saucepan, bring cereal cream, orange zest, ginger, and sugar to a boil. Remove from heat and allow to steep for 20 minutes. Set aside.

2. Chop the chocolate and melt over a double boiler (see general instructions on melting). Remove from heat when melted.

3. Strain the cream mixture and return it to the heat until the cream is scalded.

4. Pour the cream mixture over the chocolate mixture and stir.

5. Cube the butter and stir in; serve the sauce warm.

Macadamia Nut Kona Coffee Chocolate Pot de Creme

Makes eight 6-ounce servings.

2 cups	heavy cream	500 mL
2 cups	whole milk	500 mL
1	vanilla bean, split	
2 oz	Kona coffee beans, coarsely ground	55 g
4 oz	warm toasted macadamia nuts	114 g
5	egg yolks	
3	eggs	
6 oz	granulated sugar	175 mL
	fine sieve	
5- or 6-ounce	8 souffle cups	150 or 170 mL
	roasting pan	
	strainer	

1. In a heavy saucepan, scald the heavy cream, milk, nuts, coarsely ground coffee beans, and split vanilla bean. Remove from heat and allow to steep for 20 minutes, then strain through a fine sieve.

2. In a bowl, whip the egg yolks, whole eggs, and sugar until all ingredients are combined.

3. Carefully stir the cooled cream mixture into the egg mixture; then strain again.

4. Divide the mixture into the 8 small souffle cups. Place the cups in a roasting pan and add enough hot water to the pan so that it reaches three-fourths of the way up the sides of the souffle cups. Lightly cover the cups with a sheet of aluminum foil, but do not seal the top of the pan; make sure steam can escape.

5. Bake in a 525°F (160°C) oven for 45 minutes. The custard is done when it has set three-fourths of the way. The center should jiggle and still appear soupy.

6. Remove the custards from the roasting pan and place them on a dry surface for an hour. When they reach room temperature, place them in the fridge for 4 hours or more.

Chocolate Mousse Torte with Strawberries

Makes 8 servings.

1	chocolate cake	
16 oz	strawberries	500 mL
16 oz	whipping cream	500 mL
1 tsp	vanilla extract	5 mL
10 oz	dark chocolate	285 g
6	large egg yolks	
½ cup	sugar	125 mL
2 T	orange-flavored liqueur	30 mL
10-inch	spring-form pan	25 cm
	whisk	

1. Cut the cake into ½-inch (9 mm) layers. Line the bottom of the spring-form pan with a layer of chocolate cake. Arrange a layer of halved fresh strawberries over the cake. Alternate layers of cake and strawberries.

2. In a mixing bowl, whip the cream and vanilla together until the cream forms soft peaks. Set it aside.

3. Chop and melt the chocolate over a double boiler, and remove it from the heat (see general melting instructions).

4. Whip the eggs and sugar until pale yellow and fluffy, then add the orange-flavored liqueur with a whisk.

5. Carefully fold the melted chocolate into the egg mixture and blend slowly until thoroughly combined.

6. Fold in the whipped cream to the mixture; then pour it over the prepared cake in the spring-form pan. Place it in the fridge for 4 hours before serving.

Contrary to popular belief, fondue does not get its name because you are FOND of chocolate and you are DUE a treat. It really means something that is melted, from the French fondre, *to melt. Here are two great recipes passed along to us by our friends. Fondues are great for parties!*

Leslie's Fondue

This recipe comes from our friend Leslie Johnstone, who swears by it.

16–24 oz	semisweet chocolate	455–684 g
1 cup	whole milk	250 mL
1½ cups	condensed milk	375 mL
1 T	liqueur (optional)*	15 mL
	fresh fruit, such as 2 bananas, 1 apple, 2 cups (500 mL) strawberries, 2 kiwi, 1 orange, grapes	
	marshmallows (optional)	
	fondue pot, skewers, heater	

*Choose a liqueur such as orange, almond, coffee, or peppermint.

1. Chop the chocolate and heat the chocolate pieces, milk, and condensed milk over medium heat until the chocolate is melted. Stir well to mix. If you wish, add the liqueur; then mix well.

2. Cut the fruit into bite-sized pieces and put the fruit on a plate near where the fondue will be served.

3. Pour the melted chocolate mixture into the fondue pot; keep it warm.

4. Let each person place fruit on a skewer and dip it into the warm chocolate.

Katie's Fondue

Another great fondue comes from Vicki's sister in San Francisco. We know you'll love this as much as we do.

16–24 oz	semisweet chocolate, chopped	455–684 g
1½ cups	cereal cream (half and half)	375 mL
¾ cup	sugar	175 mL
	medium-sized pot	
	fresh fruit as for Leslie's Fondue, or marshmallows	
	fondue pot, forks, skewers, heater	

1. Heat the chocolate, cream, and sugar on medium heat until the chocolate is melted and the sugar dissolved.

2. Pour the melted chocolate mixture into the fondue pot; keep it warm.

3. Let each person place fruit or marshmallows on a skewer and dip them into the warm chocolate, and then eat them.

Shawn's Fondue

While I was helping out at my son's school, one of the very thin employees offered us this fattening recipe. It hasn't affected his weight any, but I don't know why. Make it during a party and serve immediately.

2.2 lb	Belgian chocolate	1 kg
6 oz	milk chocolate	170 g
2 oz	white chocolate	56 g
6 T	2%-fat milk, or cream, or more, to taste	90 mL
4	large, tart apples	
1	loaf of french bread	
1 lb	shortbread cookies	455 g
	fondue pot, skewers, heater	

1. Chop all the chocolate. Over a double boiler with hot (not boiling) water, add all the chopped chocolate.

2. Warm slowly and stir frequently. The more slowly the mixture is warmed, the creamier it will be, and the less likely to become lumpy.

3. Cut the apples and bread in bite-size pieces. Use fondue forks to dip the apples, bread, and cookies into the chocolate.

A CHOCOLATE-TASTING PARTY

If you're looking for a unique party idea, how about a chocolate tasting? It's not as pretentious as a wine tasting, and you don't have to know anything about chocolate to enjoy yourself. Have each of your guests bring several pieces of good quality chocolate. Ask them to record the brand and the price. Chop the chocolate up into small serving samples and place on a plate labeled "Type A, B," etc. Make sure you record which chocolate is on which plate, or you might have to start again. (That would really be a shame.) Create a chart and have the guests vote on the flavor, texture, color, smell, etc., of each product.

What chocolate book would be complete without a brownie recipe? Brownies are wonderful desserts for lunchboxes and for picnics.

Charlie's Brownies

After coming home late at night from work, Vicki's husband is always poking through the kitchen in the hope of finding something sweet to eat. He is overjoyed when he discovers a hidden cache of these treats. Serve with ice cream and hot fudge for a special dessert.

8 oz	butter or margarine	227 g
2 cups	sugar	500 mL
1 tsp	vanilla	5 mL
4	eggs	
1 cup	cocoa	250 mL
1 cup	all-purpose white flour	250 mL
½ tsp	baking powder	2.5 mL
pinch	salt	
13 × 9″	greased baking pan	33 × 22 cm
1½ cups	chopped walnuts or pecans (optional)	375 mL
2 oz	chocolate chips (optional)	60 mL
2 oz	whipped cream (optional)	60 mL
	large microwavable mixing bowl	

1. Preheat the oven to 350°F (177°C).

2. Melt the margarine or butter in a mixing bowl in the microwave or over low heat on the stove.

3. Remove from the microwave or pot and add in the sugar and vanilla. Stir.

4. Add the eggs in one at a time, stirring after each one.

5. Mix in cocoa, flour, baking powder, and salt and beat well. If you are adding nuts, do it now.

6. Pour the batter into the baking pan and bake 30 -35 minutes. The brownies are ready when they pull away from the edges of the pan.

7. Remove the brownies from the oven and cool completely before cutting into squares.

8. Optional: Melt the chocolate chips (see general directions); drizzle over the top of the cooled brownies. Serve with the whipped cream on the side.

Fudgy Brownies

Really gooey and messy, these are favorites with adults.

4 oz	butter or margarine	114 g
3 oz	unsweetened chocolate	85 g
2	eggs	
1 cup	granulated or brown sugar	250 mL
¾ cup	pastry flour	175 mL
pinch	salt	
1 tsp	vanilla	5 mL
1 cup	chopped walnuts (optional)	250 mL
½ cup	chocolate chips: semisweet, milk, or white	125 mL
9″ × 9″	baking pan	23 × 23 cm

1. Melt the chocolate and add the shortening; see the general melting instructions.

2. In a large mixing bowl, beat the eggs and sugar until they are light yellow and frothy. Add vanilla and the cooled chocolate mixture, and beat until blended.

3. Use a wooden spoon to add and mix the flour and salt into the chocolate/egg mixture.

4. Add the nuts and chocolate chips to the batter and pour it into the greased baking pan. Bake at 325°F (170°C) for about 25 minutes.

The store is closed and you are dying for some chocolate candy. What can you do? There's an easy solution at hand! Following these simple directions, you can solve your problem.

Chocolate Bark

You've heard of bark from a tree and have heard a dog bark, but how about chocolate bark? Here is one candy whose bark is as good as its bite.

8 oz	your favorite chocolate	227 g
1 tsp	butter or margarine	5 mL
1 cup	toasted almonds	250 mL
	cookie sheet or tray	
	waxed paper	

1. Follow the basic instructions in the general information section for melting and tempering chocolate.

2. Spread the tempered, cooled chocolate onto a cookie sheet covered with waxed paper and stir in the almonds.

3. Allow to cool and break into pieces.

Carob Snacks

Some people are allergic to chocolate or cocoa butter. There's still a treat these people can enjoy instead of chocolate. Carob, available in health food stores, is a healthy alternative to chocolate. Carob powder is made from the seed pods of an evergreen shrub that grows in the Mediterranean area. For a change, try a carob dessert, loaded with ingredients that are good for you.

1 cup	peanut butter	250 mL
1 cup	honey	250 mL
1 cup	carob powder	250 mL
1 cup	chopped walnuts, pecans, and sunflower or pumpkin seeds	250 mL
½ cup	shredded coconut	125 mL
½ cup	raisins	125 mL
1 tsp	vanilla extract	5 mL
pinch	salt	
pinch	cinnamon	

FOR DECORATING

1 cup	shredded coconut, carob chips, or confectioner's sugar	250 mL

1. Place the peanut butter and honey in a medium-sized pot and heat until the honey is runny.

2. Remove from the heat and stir in the carob powder, nuts or seeds, coconut, raisins, vanilla, salt, and cinnamon. Use a wooden spoon to mix, or knead the mixture with your hands.

3. Wet your hands and roll the mixture into small balls. To decorate, dip in coconut, confectioner's sugar, or melted carob chips. Chill in the refrigerator until hard.

Franklin Mints

Certain flavors seem to be made for each other. There's nothing quite like the marriage of rich, dark chocolate and cool mint.

INGREDIENTS

1 lb	confectioner's sugar	455 g
pinch	cream of tartar	
1	egg white	
	water	
a few drops	peppermint extract	
	green food coloring (optional)	
6 oz	semisweet chocolate	170 mL
1 T	butter or margarine	15 mL
	food processor	
	rolling pin	
	round cookie cutter or small wineglass	
	wire rack	

1. Place about two-thirds of the confectioner's sugar in the bowl of a food processor with a plastic blade.

2. Add the egg white and a pinch of the cream of tartar to the confectioner's sugar.

3. With the food processor running, add water, a teaspoon at a time to the mixture, until the mixture forms a thick ball. Add several drops of peppermint extract and mix.

4. If the mixture is too loose, add more confectioner's sugar as needed.

5. Sprinkle confectioner's sugar onto the counter or pastry board and place the peppermint dough on the sugar. Sprinkle the top of the dough with confectioner's sugar; then roll the dough into a thin layer with a rolling pin.

6. Cut circles out of the dough using a small, round cookie cutter or wineglass.

7. Gently place the cut circles on a rack and allow them to set.

8. Melt the chocolate, stir in the shortening, and temper, following the basic instructions for melting and tempering. Let it cool to about 89°–91°F (31.6°–32.7°C).

9. Dip peppermint circles in the cooled chocolate and place them on waxed paper to set.

HOW TO JUDGE CHOCOLATE

➤ Chocolate should be shiny. This is an indication of the amount of cocoa butter in the product.

➤ Chocolate should not have a grey or white tinge; it gets this when it has not been stored correctly or is not fresh.

➤ Chocolate should melt in your hand.

➤ Chocolate should break with a clean edge and not a ragged one.

➤ Chocolate should smell like, well, chocolate—not too bitter and not too sweet.

➤ Ask the salesperson where the chocolate was made, where the beans came from, and what the cocoa butter content of the chocolate is. Ask what preservatives or additives are in the product.

Chocolate Tears

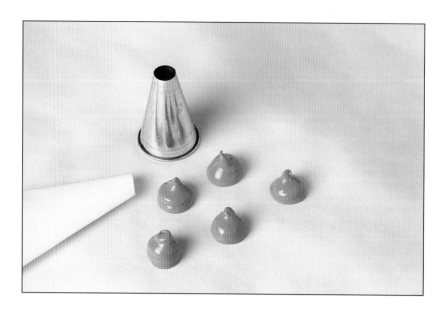

How about making a blue chocolate tear, or even a chocolate-colored one? Here's something you won't cry over. This is a great activity to do with your child on a rainy day. If you want to get really fancy, you can make the tears one color of chocolate, and then dip the hardened chocolate into another color of chocolate.

8 oz	white or semisweet chocolate	227 g
1 tsp	butter or margarine	5 mL
	powdered blue food coloring*	
	thick freezer sandwich bag, cake decorating bag or tube, or chopstick	
	waxed paper	

Note: If you use liquid food coloring, it will cause your chocolate to seize or go grainy. Add a little solid vegetable shortening to smooth out the texture of the chocolate if you use liquid food coloring; even so, the texture will not be as good.

1. Melt the chocolate, add the shortening and food coloring, and temper the mixture following the melting and tempering instructions.

2. Fill a cake decorating bag or tube with the tempered chocolate. Note: If you don't have a cake decorating bag, you can make your own. Use a spatula to scoop the melted chocolate into a thick sandwich bag. Carefully squeeze the chocolate into a corner of the bag, so the bag now resembles a cone.

3. Cover the cookie sheet with waxed paper. Cut a small hole in a corner of the bag and carefully squeeze the chocolate onto the waxed paper in tear-shaped blobs.

4. *Alternate method of making tears:* Gather chocolate up onto a chopstick and drop it onto waxed paper in blobs.

5. Put the cookie sheet in the fridge; let the tears harden; then wrap in colored plastic wrap.

Turtledoves

If you get a craving for a certain kind of store-bought chocolates, but don't feel like buying a large box, here's a way to satisfy your craving.

16 oz	caramels	455 g
1 cup	whole pecans	250 mL
16 oz	chocolate (semisweet, milk, or white)	455 g
1 tsp	butter or margarine	5 mL
	cookie sheet	

1. Spread the pecans on a cookie sheet and roast in a 350°F (177°C) oven for about 5 minutes.

2. Arrange the pecans on the same cookie sheet in groups of 4 or 5. Place one or two caramels over the nuts, depending on how "thick" you like your candy.

3. Return the caramel-covered pecans to the oven and bake for about 5–7 minutes, or until the caramels are soft.

4. Remove the cookie sheet from the oven and flatten the caramels with the back of a wooden spoon. Allow the caramels to cool and harden.

5. Melt the chocolate, stir in the shortening, and temper, following the general instructions. Let the tempered chocolate cool to about 86°–89°F (30°–31.6°C).

6. Dip the cooled caramel pecans in the chocolate to coat them, and place them on waxed paper to set.

Easy Truffles

These truffles aren't the mysterious things that pigs are trained to sniff out in the forest. Truffles are, in fact, a very adult kind of chocolate. These delicious morsels make great gifts for special occasions, and are easy to make.

½ cup	unsweetened cocoa powder	125 mL
1½ cups	confectioner's sugar	375 mL
¼ lb	unsalted butter or margarine at room temperature	114 g
	plastic wrap	
	melon baller or teaspoon	

FOR DECORATING

½ cup	unsweetened cocoa powder	125 mL
½ cup	confectioner's sugar	125 mL

1. Place ½ cup cocoa, 1½ cups of confectioner's sugar, and the shortening in a mixer and mix until ingredients are fluffy and smooth.

2. Cover the bowl with plastic wrap and put the bowl in the fridge for at least one hour.

3. Roll the mixture into tiny balls, using either the melon baller or a teaspoon and your fingers. If the mixture gets too soft, return it to the fridge to harden before decorating.

4. Roll the cold balls in unsweetened cocoa or more confectioner's sugar.

5. Store the finished balls in plastic wrap and leave them in the refrigerator for special occasions—like, the kids have gone to bed.

Milk Chocolate Balls

What would life be without chocolate and, in particular, milk chocolate? Make your own with this easy recipe. *Makes 24 balls.*

8 oz	finely chopped milk chocolate	227 g
4 oz	unsalted butter or margarine	114 g
3	large eggs	
	wax-paper-covered tray	
	melon baller or teaspoon	

FOR DIPPING

16–24 oz	milk chocolate or other high-quality chocolate	455–680 g
	thermometer	

1. Place the 8 oz of milk chocolate in a medium-size microwavable dish. Melt the chocolate in 20-second bursts of the microwave, stirring after each microwaving. Do not overcook.

2. Remove from the microwave and immediately beat in the butter or margarine.

3. Separate the yolks from the whites of the eggs. Add the yolks, one at a time, to the chocolate mixture, stirring between each egg.

4. Cover the mixture and place it in the fridge until firm.

5. Remove it from the fridge and roll the mixture into tiny balls, using either a melon baller or a teaspoon.

6. Place these balls in the freezer until they are frozen solid.

7. Melt and temper the chocolate for dipping, following the general instructions for melting and tempering. Do not try to roll the balls in the melted chocolate until the chocolate is properly tempered .The dipping chocolate should be between 86° and 89°F (30° and 31.6°C). Take a few balls from the freezer at a time, and working quickly, roll the balls in the chocolate to coat. Place the dipped chocolates on the wax-paper-covered tray. Store them in the fridge.

Aunt Doba Lee's Dipped Fruit

What could be tastier than the combination of chocolate and fruit? *Makes 4 servings.*

16 oz	fruit such as strawberries, cherries, kiwis, pears, apples, or pineapple	455 g
8 oz	white chocolate	227 g
8 oz	semisweet dark chocolate	227 g
1 T	butter or margarine	15 mL
	wax-paper-covered tray	

1. Wash and dry the fruit. Make sure there is no water on the work surface you will be using for dipping.

2. Keeping the white and dark chocolates in separate bowls, melt each chocolate and stir in the shortening; temper each, following the directions in the general instructions section. Cool the chocolate to 86°–89°F (30°–31.6°C).

3. Dip the fruit in one kind of chocolate and allow it to set on waxed paper. Dip the other side of the fruit in the second kind of chocolate after the first side has set. Store in the refrigerator.

Candied Fruit Peels

Here's another fruit-based candy recipe with a delicious combination of tart and sweet flavors.

1 cup	water	250 mL
1 cup	sugar	250 mL
1 or 2	small oranges or lemons (or dried apricots, ginger or other prepared fruit)	
1 T	butter or margarine	15 mL
16 oz	semisweet chocolate	455 g
	toothpicks	
	wax-paper-covered tray	

1. Carefully peel the skin from the lemons and oranges; cut the peels in strips. Place the peels in boiling water for about 5 minutes.

2. Remove the peels from the boiling water, and immediately place them in a bowl of ice water.

3. Place the peels in fresh boiling water for another few minutes, then back into a bowl of ice water.

4. Bring 1 cup of sugar and 1 cup of water to boil in a heavy saucepan. When the sugar has dissolved, add the fruit peels and simmer over low heat until the peel has absorbed the sugar, stirring constantly.

5. Dry the peel on a wire rack.

6. Melt the chocolate, stir in the shortening, and temper following the general melting and tempering instructions. Cool the chocolate to 86°–89°F (30–31.6°C).

7. Dip each piece of fruit peel in the chocolate, using a toothpick as a holder. Place on the waxed paper to set. Dip the dried fruit in the same way.

THE CHOCOLATE BUFFET:
Recipes from the Sutton Place Restaurant

For many years Vancouverites have been enjoying the Chocoholic Bar offered by the Sutton Place Hotel, an all-you-can-eat chocolate buffet. The authors have eaten so much at this buffet that the next day we had a "chocolate hangover." Chef Wolfgang Dauke has been kind enough to share three of the most popular of the desserts he has created with us. Since we're not all lucky enough to live in Vancouver, here's a way to enjoy these treats at home.

Chocolate Brownie Fruit Pizza

According to the chef, this is the dessert most requested by the movie stars who stay at the Sutton Place Hotel. *Makes 8 servings.*

½ lb	butter	227 g
2 cups	sugar	500 mL
4	eggs	
½ cup	dark unsweetened cocoa	125 mL
¾ cup	cake flour	175 mL
1½ tsp	baking powder	7.5 mL
10″	quiche pan	25 cm
16 oz	seasonal fruits, sliced into bite-sized pieces	455 g
4 oz	white chocolate for curls	114 g

1. To make the brownie base, combine the butter and sugar and add the eggs one at a time. Mix until fluffy.

2. Add the cocoa, flour, and baking powder to the mixture, and blend.

3. Pour the batter into the quiche pan and bake for 10 minutes at 350°F (177°C).

4. Cool the brownie base. Place the fruit on top of the brownie base.

5. Shave white chocolate curls and sprinkle on top for "cheese."

Chocolate Paté

Here is another popular recipe from the Sutton Place Hotel. *Makes 8 servings.*

24 oz	dark couverture chocolate	680 g
1 cup	whipping cream	250 mL
13	egg yolks	
6 oz	softened butter	170 g
2 T	orange-flavored liqueur	30 mL
4 × 9 in.	2 terrine molds or full-size (6 cup) bread loaf pans	10 × 23 cm
1 cup	fruit or pureed raspberries for topping	250 mL

1. Melt the chocolate in a double boiler.

2. In a separate pan, bring the cream to a simmer; then add the egg yolks and cook until the mixture coats the back of a spoon; this is called the "rose stage."

3. Add butter and melted chocolate to the ingredients in Step 2 and stir well to combine all ingredients.

4. Pour the mixture into two terrine molds or loaf pans and refrigerate overnight.

5. Serve thin slices of the paté topped with fruit or pureed raspberries.

Chocolate Truffle Cake

Here is one of our favorite party desserts from Chef Wolfgang Dauke of the Sutton Place Hotel, Vancouver. *Makes one 12-inch cake.*

9 oz	dark couverture chocolate	255 g
3 oz	sugar	90 mL
6	egg yolks	
1 T	mint-flavored liqueur	15 mL
1⅔ cup	whipping cream	415 mL
12″ diameter	1 store-bought white or chocolate sponge cake	30 cm diameter
12″ diameter	1 spring-form pans	30 cm
3 oz	block of chocolate for curls	85 g

1. Melt the chocolate in the top of a double boiler. Leave it over hot water so it stays melted.

2. In another pot, boil the sugar with a small amount of water until it reaches the soft-ball stage, 234°F (112°C).

3. Whip the egg yolks until they are yellow and fluffy, then add the sugar mixture to the egg yolks. Continue mixing until it reaches room temperature.

4. Whip the cream; set it aside.

5. Fold the melted chocolate and liqueur into the egg/sugar mixture; then fold in the whipped cream.

6. Place the sponge cake in the bottom of the spring-form pan. Pour the chocolate and cream mixture onto the sponge cake. Refrigerate overnight and decorate with chocolate curls (see general instructions for making chocolate curls).

WEIRD CHOCOLATE

If you are looking for something really unusual to make for a treat, here are several tasty but silly chocolate recipes. These delights are guaranteed to raise eyebrows.

Chocolate-covered swizzle sticks make a tasty party favor. See Chocolate Spoon recipe.

Mom's Chow Mein Haystacks

This is one of the easiest and simplest treats around. It has been a favorite of children for the last 40 years. Our mothers, Dorothy Levine and Florence Lorber-Parecki, always made these for special occasions. Thanks, Mom. *Makes 2 dozen haystacks.*

8 oz	chocolate chips	227 g
8 oz	butterscotch chips	227 g
1½ cups	chow mein noodles	375 mL
1 tsp	butter or margarine	5 mL
½ cup	shelled walnut pieces	125 mL
¼ cup	crushed toffee pieces (optional)	60 mL
	waxed paper	

1. Place both kinds of chips in a large, microwavable bowl, or in the top of a double boiler. Warm the chips until they have just begun to melt.

2. Remove the chips from the heat, add butter or margarine, and stir until chips are melted.

3. Add the chow mein noodles, walnuts, and crushed toffee pieces to the melted chips, and stir to cover the noodles.

4. Scoop out spoonfuls of the mixture and place it on waxed paper in a pile (see photo). Place the finished haystacks in the fridge to harden.

Chocolate Pretzels

This is a great gift to make for Father's Day. Have your children surprise Dad with chocolate pretzels to munch on during his favorite sports game. *Makes 2 dozen large pretzels.*

14 oz.	long, thick pretzels*	396 g
16 oz	your favorite kind of chocolate	455 g
1 tsp	butter or margarine	5 mL
	waxed paper	

*Don't use the thin, short ones as they break when dipped.

1. Melt the chocolate, stir in the butter or margarine, and temper following the general instructions on melting and tempering. Cool to 86°–89°F (30°–31.6°C).
2. Hold a pretzel by one end and roll or dip it in the warm chocolate.

3. Gently lay the dipped pretzel on a tray covered with waxed paper.
4. Place finished pretzels in the fridge until they are fully hardened; store in a plastic container in a cool, dark place.

Chocolate Potato Chips

You might want to work with a friend to make these treats. While you are dipping the dark side, have your friend start on a pile of chips for the white side. You probably won't need to store these chips, as you will have finished eating them by the time they have hardened. *Makes 2 to 4 servings.*

9 oz	**thick, ridged dipping type of potato chips**	250 g
8 oz	**dark chocolate**	227 g
8 oz	**white chocolate**	227 g
2 tsp	**butter or margarine**	10 mL
	waxed paper	

1. Melt the dark chocolate and stir in 1 teaspoon of the butter or margarine, and temper, following the instructions in the general directions. Cool to 86°–89°F (30°–31.6°C).

2. Repeat Step 1 with the white chocolate.

3. Dip each potato chip halfway into the dark chocolate, place it on the waxed paper, and allow to set.

4. When the dark sides have set, dip the other sides of the chips into the white chocolate. Allow to set on waxed paper.

Chocolate Matzos

For Jewish children around the world, Passover is a special time. Children can hardly wait to eat matzo, a flat baked type of cracker, which is eaten instead of bread. Here is a Passover recipe that will please your family. *Makes 8 matzos.*

12 oz	dark chocolate	340 g
2 tsp	butter or margarine	10 mL
8	unsalted matzos	
	paintbrush	
	thermometer	

1. Melt the dark chocolate, stir in the butter or margarine, and temper as described in the general directions. If you cannot find any cooking chocolate, you can use cocoa and and butter or margarine.

2. Paint one side of the matzo with chocolate.

Snowballs

Here's a recipe for a snowball you won't want to throw at anyone. *Makes 18 snowballs.*

1 cup	mashed potatoes	250 mL
1 cup	confectioner's sugar	250 mL
a few drops	peppermint extract	
8 oz	semisweet chocolate	227 g
1 tsp	butter or margarine	5 mL

FOR DECORATIONS

2 cups	coconut	500 mL
1 cup	cocoa powder or semisweet chocolate	250 mL

1. Mix the mashed potatoes, confectioner's sugar, and peppermint in a large mixing bowl.

2. Roll the mixture into small balls and freeze.

3. Roll the frozen balls in prepared melted chocolate, or cocoa powder. Decorate with coconut.

Chicken Mole

If you're looking at the word *mole* and thinking that you are going to be cooking a mole, an animal that lives in tunnels in the ground, you are mistaken. Mole is a special kind of Mexican sauce, pronounced *moe lay*. It comes from a Nahuatl word meaning a sauce or stew. A sweet mole made with bitter chocolate is called *mole poblano*. You can place this delicious sauce over baked chicken and stun your family with your gourmet cooking. It is also a wonderful way to use some leftover chicken or turkey. *Makes 4 servings.*

4-lb	roasted chicken or turkey	2 kg
1 heaping tsp	minced garlic	5 mL
	large, ripe banana	
⅓ cup	pitted prunes	75 mL
¼ cup	raisins	60 mL
1 T	creamy peanut butter	15 mL
¼ cup	water	60 mL
1	large, finely chopped onion	
⅓ cup	unsweetened cocoa powder	75 mL
3 T	chili powder	45 mL
3 T	sugar	45 mL
½ tsp	ground cinnamon	2.5 mL
pinch of each	ground cumin	
	ground cloves	
	ground coriander	
	ground anise seeds	
2½ cups	chicken broth or soup (without noodles)	625 mL
6 oz	can of tomato paste	170 g
	blender or food processor	

1. Place garlic, banana, prunes, raisins, peanut butter and ¼ cup water in a blender or food processor and pulse the mixture until it is well blended.

2. Spoon the mixture into a large frying pan, add the onion, and cook over medium heat for about 10 minutes. Add a tablespoon (15 mL) of water if the mixture dries out.

3. Add the cocoa, chili, sugar, cinnamon, cloves, cumin, coriander, and anise to the frying pan and mix.

4. Pour in half of the chicken broth and stir until it boils.

5. Return the mixture to the blender or food processor. Add the tomato paste and some broth. Don't fill to the top, as some may spill over. Pulse the mixture until it is smooth and creamy.

6. Serve the warm mole over baked chicken or turkey, or roll up chicken pieces in a warm tortilla and top with mole.

Chocolate Spoons

In gourmet shops and cafes, you can purchase chocolate spoons or stirring sticks. These are extremely easy to make and are great gifts for both adults and children. *Makes one dozen spoons or swizzle sticks.*

12	colored plastic spoons or fancy swizzle sticks	
8 oz	milk, semisweet, or white chocolate	227 g
1 tsp	butter or margarine	5 mL
	waxed paper	
	colored cellophane wrapping	
	ribbon	

1. Melt the chocolate, stir in the shortening, and temper following the general directions on melting and tempering.

2. Cool to 86°–89°F (30°–31.6°C).

3. Coat the end of each spoon or stir stick and lay it on waxed paper to set.

4. Wrap the set chocolate treats in colored cellophane and tie them with ribbon.

From fancy to simple, here's something sure to please everyone; perfect recipes for holidays or special occasions.

Chocolate Pavlova

Most people are familiar with the traditional White Pavlova. Here's a chocolate lover's twist on this elegant dessert. *Makes 8 servings.*

INGREDIENTS

6	large egg whites	
1½ cup	fine sugar	375 mL
1 tsp	vinegar	5 mL
2 T	fine sifted flour	30 mL
¼ cup	cocoa powder	60 mL
pinch	salt	
16 oz	chocolate whipped cream	500 mL
16 oz	fruit*	500 mL

Instead of traditional kiwis, try raspberries, bing cherries or even strawberries.

Making the meringue shell.

1. Preheat the oven to 300°F (149°C). Line a cookie sheet with aluminum foil and lightly dust it with flour.

2. Beat the egg whites until they form peaks; then slowly add the fine sugar, beating after each addition.

3. Slowly add vinegar, cocoa, and salt to the egg white and gently fold until completely mixed.

4. Pipe or spoon the egg whites in a 10-inch (25 cm) circle on the foil. Build up the edges of the circle so that the meringue forms a basket or container shape.

5. Bake for ½ hour at 300°F (149°C); then turn the oven down to 250°F or (121°C) and continue to bake for another 1½ hours.

6. Remove from the oven and cool on a wire rack before filling.

7. Fill the meringue Pavlova shell with the chocolate whipped cream (see recipe, next page) and decorate the Pavlova with sliced fruit.

Chocolate Whipped Cream

You can make this for the Chocolate Pavlova filling or to decorate other desserts.

6 T	unsweetened cocoa powder	90 mL
¾ cup	confectioner's sugar	175 mL
1 tsp	vanilla	5 mL
16 oz	whipping cream	500 mL

1. Place all the ingredients in a large bowl and stir to mix. Put the mixture in the fridge for at least 1 hour.

2. Whip the mixture until stiff. Caution: Do not overwhip or it will turn to butter.

—·—·—·—·—·—·—·—·—·—·—·—·—·—·—

Chocolate Mousse Cake

This recipe is from pastry chef Marc Tilken, president of Van Den Bosch Patisserie Belge & Bakery, Ltd. of Vancouver, Canada. *Makes 10 servings.*

9 in	chocolate sponge cake	22 cm
9 in	spring-form pan	22 cm
¼ cup	cocoa	60 mL
	pastry brush	

FOR THE MOUSSE

8 oz	dark chocolate	227 g
½ cup	butter	125 mL
4	egg yolks	
¾ cup	egg whites	175 mL
¼ cup	sugar	60 mL
¼ cup	liqueur (e.g., Grand Marnier)	60 mL

FOR THE LIQUEUR-FLAVORED SYRUP

8 oz	water	250 mL
¾ cup	sugar	175 g
2 T (appx.)	liqueur (e.g., Grand Marnier)	30 mL

1. Make a sugar syrup by mixing 8 oz (250 mL) of water with ¾ cup sugar (175 g) and boiling it until all the sugar is dissolved, stirring continuously. Mix in Grand Marnier or the liqueur of your choice in the ratio of 8 parts sugar syrup to 1 part liqueur (about 2 T). Brush the layers of cake in the liqueur-flavored syrup, using the pastry brush. Set them aside.

TO MAKE THE MOUSSE

2. Melt the dark chocolate over warm water at 122°F (50°C). Add the butter and stir until it is melted.

3. Beat the egg yolks and add a little of the chocolate mixture to the beaten egg yolks. Then add the rest of the chocolate and stir.

4. Whip the egg whites with a pinch of sugar. Then add the rest of the ¼ cup of sugar and whip until firm.

5. Add the egg whites and sugar mixture to the chocolate mixture.

TO ASSEMBLE

1. Cut the sponge cake in 3 parts. Trim the cake so it is ½ inch smaller in diameter than the pan.

2. Place a layer of sponge cake in the springform pan.

3. Add a layer of mousse. Spread it until it is smooth and there are no air bubbles. Alternate layers of cake and mousse two more times.

4. Top with cocoa.

5. Refrigerate the cake for 6 hours or freeze 1 to 2 hours.

6. Use a hair dryer to warm up the springform pan for a few seconds; be sure not to overheat the cake, however. This will give it a nice, round edge. Then remove the cake from the pan. Decorate it as desired.

Mozart Cake

Here is another recipe from Marc Tilken at Van Den Bosch Patisserie Belge & Bakery, Ltd., of Vancouver, Canada. *Makes 10 servings.*

9-in	spring-form pan	22.5 cm
8 oz	white chocolate	227 g
2 cups	whipping cream	500 mL
¼ cup	Irish liqueur for cake	60 mL
	pastry brush	
9-in	white sponge cake (store-bought), sliced in 3 thin layers	

FOR THE LIQUEUR FLAVORED SYRUP

8 oz	water	250 mL
¾ cup	sugar	175 g
2 T (appx.)	Irish liqueur	30 mL

FOR DECORATING THE CAKE

4 oz	white chocolate	114 g
1 oz	dark chocolate	30 g
1 tsp	butter or margarine	1.25 mL

1. Melt the chocolate over warm water at 122°F (50°C). Be sure the temperature of the chocolate doesn't go above this or it will turn grainy.

2. To make the mousse, whip the cream to soft peaks and add ⅓ of the cream to the chocolate. Then add the rest of the cream, plus the ¼ cup of the liqueur, to the chocolate, a little bit at a time, mixing slowly by hand. Don't overmix.

3. Make the liqueur-flavored syrup by mixing ¾ cup (175 g) of sugar with 8 oz (250 mL) of water and boiling it until all the sugar is dissolved. Mix in Irish liqueur or the liqueur of your choice in the ratio of 8 parts sugar syrup to 1 part liqueur.

4. Brush the sponge cake with the liqueur-flavored syrup mixture, using a pastry brush.
5. Put a layer of sponge cake in the bottom of the spring-form pan. Add a layer of mousse on top.
6. Continue alternating cake and mousse.
7. Refrigerate the cake for 6 hours or freeze it for 2 hours. Use a hair dryer to heat it enough to remove it from the cake pan. It should be heated for a few seconds only.
8. Decorate with white chocolate shavings or your favorite white icing. See the Doodles recipe and make musical notes for decoration out of the dark chocolate.

White Chocolate Amaretto Mousse

This recipe makes a wonderful spring dessert. Decorate with candied violets, roses, or nasturtiums, or chocolate shavings. *Makes 4 servings.*

8 oz	white baking chocolate	227 g
5 T	boiling water	75 mL
4	large eggs, separated	
1 T	almond extract	15 mL
3 T	amaretto or similar liqueur	45 mL
1 cup	whipping cream	250 mL
4	dessert bowls	

FOR GARNISH

4 oz	roasted almonds	113 g
4 oz	fruit, sliced	113 g

1. Place the white chocolate in a food processor with a chopping blade and process until the chocolate is finely broken down (about 5 minutes).
2. While the food processor is on, pour in the boiling water and continue to process until the chocolate is thick and creamy.
3. Add the egg yolks, the almond extract, and the liqueur, and process for 1 minute. Pour the mixture into a large bowl.
4. Beat the egg whites until stiff and fold them into the chocolate mixture.
5. Beat whipping cream and gently fold it into the egg white–chocolate mixture. Pour it into individual dessert dishes and place them in the fridge for several hours.
6. Before serving, garnish with roasted almonds and fresh fruit.

Lisa's Chocolate Biscotti

Kids love dipping cookies into milk. As adults, we, of course, cannot participate in such simple delights without looking immature. Instead, we dip adult cookies in coffee. This is considered European and sophisticated. Go figure. *Makes 16 biscotti.*

FOR THE BISCOTTI

2 cups	all-purpose flour	500 mL
½ cup	unsweetened cocoa powder	125 mL
1 tsp	baking soda	5 mL
1 tsp	salt	5 mL
3 oz	unsalted butter	85 g
1 cup	superfine sugar	250 mL
2	large eggs	
1 cup	roasted, chopped walnuts or pecans	250 mL
6 oz	semisweet chocolate chips	170 g
	cookie sheet	
	rack	

FOR COATING

1 T	confectioner's sugar (optional)	15 mL
8 oz	semisweet chocolate (optional) plus	227 g
1 T	butter or margarine	15 mL

1. Preheat oven to 350°F (177°C). In a medium-size bowl, whisk together flour, cocoa, baking soda, and salt.

2. In a larger bowl, beat the butter and fine sugar until fluffy and smooth.

3. Add eggs to the butter and sugar mixture and beat for 1 minute.

4. Stir in the dry ingredients from Step 1 and beat until it forms a stiff dough. Stir in the nuts and chocolate chips.

5. Divide the dough and place on a greased and lightly floured cookie sheet.

6. Form the dough into two 12 × 2 inch logs (30 × 5 cm) on the sheet.

7. Bake for 35 minutes at 350°F (177°C); then remove from oven and allow to sit for 5 minutes on the cookie sheet. Cut in ¾ inch (2 cm) slices and cook for another 10 minutes. Cool on rack.

8. When biscotti have cooled, you can dust them with confectioner's sugar or dip them in your favorite melted and tempered chocolate to coat them (see general instructions on melting and tempering).

Chocolate Pots

This is an adaptation of a dessert served at a popular restaurant in Vancouver. The chocolate pots are a big hit at formal dinner parties. *Makes 6 pots.*

FOR DOUBLE CHOCOLATE MOUSSE

4 oz	dark chocolate	113 g
4 oz	milk chocolate	113 g
4 tsp	butter	20 mL
1 T	brandy	15 mL
6	egg yolks	
4 tsp	sugar	20 mL
1¼ cup	whipping cream	300 mL
	food processor	

FOR POTS

8 oz	6 custard cups or unglazed clay flowerpots*	250 mL
6	carnations	
18	store bought flat, round chocolate cookies	
1 cup	whipping cream (optional)	250 mL

Don't use glazed flowerpots as some glazes may have lead in them.

TO MAKE THE MOUSSE

1. Chop the dark and milk chocolate and melt together over low heat. Add the butter to the melted chocolate.

2. In a food processor, whip the yolks and sugar until the mixture is thick and yellow; then add brandy and mix again.

3. Slowly add the slightly cooled, melted chocolate to the egg yolk mixture and mix for 1 minute. Scrape down the food processor and mix again.

4. Whip the cream until it is stiff and fold in the chocolate mixture.

TO ASSEMBLE AND SERVE

1. Place a chocolate cookie over the hole in the bottom of each small flower pot.

2. Fill the pot with the mousse.

3. Crumble chocolate wafers over the top of the mousse to resemble earth.

4. Place the mousse in the fridge to set.

5. Remove the pots from the fridge just before serving and place a carnation in the center of each pot. Serve with whipped cream on the side.

Note: as clay is very porous, be sure to wash and scrub the pots well after using them with hot, soapy water.

Coffee Liqueur Torte

You may wish to keep the recipe for this dessert handy, because everyone will want to know how to make it. Our friend Leslie Lambert first made this one about 10 years ago, and we have her to thank for this recipe. If you are watching your calories or cholesterol, you can substitute any nondairy whipped topping for the cream. *Makes 8 servings.*

FOR COOKIE BASE

4 oz	softened butter	114 g
½ cup	white sugar	125 mL
¼ cup	brown sugar	60 mL
1	egg	
1 tsp	vanilla	5 mL
1¼ cup	flour	300 mL
2 tsp	unsweetened cocoa powder	10 mL
½ tsp	baking soda	2.5 mL
6 oz	chopped semisweet chocolate	170 g
½ cup	chopped walnuts or pecans	125 mL

FOR FILLING

16 oz	whipping cream	500 mL
½ cup	coffee-flavored liqueur	125 mL
½ cup	milk	125 mL
1 cup	toffee bits	250 mL
1 tsp	instant coffee	5 mL
	cookie sheet	
8-inch	spring-form pan	20 cm

COOKIE BATTER

1. Preheat the oven to 350°F (177°C). Cream the butter and sugars, then add in the egg and vanilla. Beat again until smooth. Set aside.
2. In a large bowl, combine the flour, cocoa powder, and baking soda.
3. Add the butter mixture to the dry ingredients and mix.
4. Stir in the nuts and the chocolate pieces and mix to make the cookie batter.
5. Press a thin layer of the cookie batter onto the bottom of the spring-form pan. Using the bottom layer as a pattern, press out another thin layer of cookie batter on the cookie sheet to form an 8-inch-round (20 cm) cookie.
6. Bake both the cookies about 25 minutes at 350°F (177°C), or until done.
7. While the cookie on the cookie sheet is still warm and soft, trim the edges so that it will exactly fit inside the spring-form pan. Save the cookie crumbs for the top of the torte.

FILLING

To make the filling, add the instant coffee to the whipping cream and beat until stiff.

TO ASSEMBLE

1. Place the milk and coffee liqueur in a large, wide bowl or cookie sheet. Soak the cookies in the milk so the bottoms of the cookies are covered in the mixture.
2. Place one of the cookies in the bottom of the spring-form pan and drizzle a few tablespoons of the liqueur-and-milk mixture on top of the cookie. Cover the cookie with a layer of coffee-flavored whipped cream, then sprinkle with the toffee pieces.
3. Carefully place the second soaked cookie over the whipped cream, then cover with the remaining whipped cream. Sprinkle with toffee bits and cookie crumbs.
4. Cover the pan with plastic wrap and leave in the fridge overnight.
5. To serve, run a hot knife around the inside rim of the spring-form pan; then gently open the pan.

Chocolate Mousse Pie

After a light meal, it's great to indulge in a rich dessert. Here's a spectacular dinner party dessert, one you can feel guilty about eating the next morning. See the Chocolate Leaves recipe for decorations on top. *Makes 12 servings.*

FOR THE CRUST

3 cups	chocolate wafer cookie crumbs	750 mL
2 oz	softened butter	57 g
10-inch	spring-form pan	25 cm

FOR THE MOUSSE

16 oz	semisweet chocolate	455 g
2	eggs	
4	egg yolks	
4	egg whites	
2 cups	whipping cream	500 mL
6 T	confectioner's sugar	90 mL

TO MAKE THE CRUST

1. Combine the butter and cookie crumbs and press them into the bottom and sides of the spring-form pan.

2. Refrigerate for ½ hour.

TO MAKE THE MOUSSE AND ASSEMBLE

1. Melt the chocolate in the top of a double boiler.

2. Cool the chocolate; then add the whole eggs and egg yolks, mixing thoroughly. Set aside.

3. Add the confectioner's sugar to the cream, and whip until stiff. Set aside.

4. Beat the egg whites until stiff; then fold them gently into the whipped cream from Step 3.

5. Fold the egg white + whipped cream filling into the chocolate (from Step 2) until the mixtures are completely blended.

6. Pour the filling into the chilled spring-form pan, over the layer of crumbs, and place it in the fridge overnight.

7. To serve, decorate with chocolate leaves and fresh flowers.

Grasshopper Pie with Chocolate Pie Crust

There are recipes for chocolate-covered bugs, but this—mercifully—is not one of them. The chocolate pie shell can be filled with just about anything. For variety, try it with a key lime or even a lemon meringue filling. *Makes 8 servings.*

FOR PIE SHELL

1 T	butter or margarine	15 mL
6 to 8 oz	semisweet chocolate or chips	170–227 g
8 inch	pie plate	20 cm

FOR FILLING

6	egg yolks	
1 cup	sugar	250 mL
1 T	unflavored gelatin	15 mL
½ cup	cold water	125 mL
16 oz	whipping cream	500 mL
⅓ cup	creme de menthe or other liqueur	75 mL

FOR CHOCOLATE CURLS
(optional)

| 4 oz | long, wide piece of chocolate for chocolate curls | 113 g |

PIE SHELL

1. Melt the chocolate, stir in the butter or margarine, and temper, following the general instructions.

2. Smooth the melted chocolate all over the inside of an ungreased pie plate and along the rim, and place it in the fridge to harden. (You can also line the pie plate with foil, cover it with chocolate, and then peel away the foil after the chocolate has hardened.).

MAKING THE FILLING AND ASSEMBLY

3. Beat the egg yolks; then add sugar and beat them together until light and fluffy. Set it aside.

4. Place the gelatin in the top of a double boiler and add ½. cup of cold water to soften it.

5. Dissolve the gelatin over low heat; then bring to a boil.

6. Add the egg mixture to the gelatin and stir thoroughly. Remove immediately from heat.

7. When the mixture is cool, add it to the whipped cream in a bowl. Stir in the liqueur and pour the mixture into the chocolate shell.

8. Decorate with chocolate curls if desired. Make them by scraping the blade of a sharp knife along the top of a long, wide piece of chocolate that has been warmed slightly. The size of your chocolate will determine the length of your curls.

9. To cut, dip a knife in boiling water and slice the pie.

If you can't eat chocolate for breakfast, how about drinking some? Here are some simple recipes from our families that your children can make.

Joshua's Chocolate Milk Shake

Joshua hated drinking milk, but was converted when he tasted this wonderful concoction. *Makes 1 serving.*

	blender	
8 oz	milk (skim works just fine)	250 mL
1 cup	vanilla or chocolate ice cream	250 mL
½ cup	homemade or store-bought chocolate syrup*	125 mL
several	ice cubes	
handful	chocolate chips or other candy such as peanut butter bits, or half of a candy bar	

See recipe for Brian's Chocolate Syrup.

Place all the ingredients in a blender and mix until everything is smooth. Pour into a huge glass and enjoy.

— · — · — · — · — · — · — · — · — · —

Trevor's Soda

Vicki's son taught us how to make this. It's like a regular ice cream float, but with a chocolate twist. *Makes 1 serving.*

½ cup	unflavored soda water (seltzer)	125 mL
4 T	chocolate syrup*	60 mL
6 oz	vanilla or chocolate ice cream	170 g

See recipe for Brian's Chocolate Syrup.

1. Add about ½ cup or 125 mL of soda water and syrup to a glass and stir.

2. Drop ice cream into the glass and have your child slowly fill the rest of the glass with soda water. Go slowly as the soda water will bubble up.

Note: A new York egg cream is really a fancy chocolate soda. Unlike its name, it has NO egg and very little cream. Go figure! To make the egg cream, take out the ice cream and substitute ½ cup or 125 mL of cereal cream for the ice cream in the above recipe.

— · — · — · — · — · — · — · — · — · —

Shira's Hot Cocoa

When Shira arrives home wet and cold from riding her horse, she dives into a large steaming latté bowl of hot cocoa. *Makes 1 serving.*

1 cup	milk	250 mL
1 T	cocoa	15 mL
1 T	sugar	15 mL
	whipped cream, ice cream or marshmallows (optional)	
	peppermint stick or cinnamon stick (optional)	

1. Pour the milk into the mug which you want to drink from; then pour this milk into a small saucepan or small pot.

2. Heat the milk until it is very hot, but not boiling.

3. Place the cocoa and sugar in the mug and add a tablespoon or so of the hot milk. Stir quickly to make a paste and pour the hot milk into the mug and stir to mix.

4. For a richer and creamier flavor, add a dollop of whipped cream or a huge spoonful of any flavored ice cream to the top of the mug. Marshmallows, peppermint candy or cinnamon sticks make tasty toppings.

Real Hot Chocolate

To be completely decadent, you can try these variations on hot chocolate. *Makes 1 serving.*

8 oz	milk	250 mL
4 oz	chocolate bar	113 g
	egg yolk (optional)	

1. Break up about half of your favorite kind of pure chocolate bar and add to a pot of very hot milk. Stir until the chocolate is completely melted and blended with the milk. Whisk the mixture until it is smooth.

2. For a European touch, add the above mixture, a little at a time, to a beaten egg yolk. Whisk until frothy.

Mexican Hot Chocolate

If you look around specialty stores, you can find Mexican chocolate. It usually comes in round blocks and can be broken up to make a bittersweet chocolate drink. To make adult drinks, add coffee-flavored liqueur before serving. This makes a great drink to accompany the mole sauce. *Makes 4 servings.*

4–6 oz	Mexican chocolate	113–170 g
3 cups	milk	750 mL
½ cup	brown sugar	125 mL
pinch	ground cloves	
pinch	ground cinnamon	
	whipped cream or coffee-flavored ice cream (optional)	

1. Warm the milk over low heat.
2. Break up the chocolate, place in the blender, and add warm milk.
3. Pulse the blender until the chocolate is completely pureed and mixed with milk.

4. Add sugar, cloves, and cinnamon to the chocolate milk; blend for several seconds.
5. Place in mugs and serve with whipped cream or coffee-flavored ice cream, if desired.

TRIVIA

A *molinillo* is a tiny, whisklike cooking tool used by Spanish-speaking chocolate aficionados to mix the cocoa when making hot chocolate. Traditionally associated with Mexican hot chocolate, this tool is held between the palms while it is rapidly turned back and forth to create a froth.

ACKNOWLEDGMENTS

Our sincerest thanks to Diana Becker, who not only loaned us the kitchen at the Dubrelle French Cooking School, but also made her staff and students available for the photography session. We don't know what we would have done without her. Thanks also to Jay Forsyth and Aris Zouzoulas for helping with the food preparation.

Thanks to Dorothy Levine, Leslie Johnstone, Katie Lorber-Christie, Florence Lorber-Parecki, Doba Lee Harris, Leslie Lambert, Claudia Russell, Elizabeth Klaas, and Jay Forsyth for sharing their recipes. To Paul, Charlie, Josh, Shira, Trevor, Brian and Lisa, thanks for being guinea pigs. It was a tough job, but someone had to do it. And, as always, thanks, Maurice. We told you that all this chocolate eating would pay off.

The authors wish to gratefully acknowledge and thank the following chefs and businesses:

- Purdy's Chocolates, Vancouver, B.C.; a very big thank-you to Tom Cinnamon for his technical expertise; thanks also to Shelly Matheson and Neil Hastie. Our thanks for generously donating the baking chocolate and your factory for photographs. We really appreciated the lessons in the fine art of chocolatiering.
- Foley's Chocolates, Vancouver, B.C.; in particular, Martin Gagel. Thanks for allowing us to tour and photograph the production lines, explaining chocolate-making, and donating chocolates for baking and photographing.
- Sutton Place Hotel, Vancouver, B.C.; in particular, Judy Ahola and Wolfgang Dauke, Chief Pastry Chef. We gained weight at the incredible chocolate buffet. Thanks for sharing recipes!
- Puddifoots, especially Joanne Milford. Thanks for providing the beautiful dishes, glasses, and cookware and for all your time.
- Ming Wo's, especially Regan Lang. A great place for any kind of cooking utensils and kitchenware. Thanks for helping.
- Hilton Waikoloa Village, especially David Brown, Executive Pastry Chef. Thanks for everything, especially the wonderful recipes.
- Marc Tilken, pastry chef and president of Van Den Bosch Patisserie Belge & Bakery, Ltd., Vancouver, B.C., for sharing the recipes for the Chocolate Mousse Cake and the Mozart Cake with us.
- Charles Sigvardsen, founder of Charlie's Chocolate Factory Ltd., Burnaby and Port Coquitlam, B.C., for instructions on and photographs of molding chocolates.
- Shawn Eades, who shared his time and sculpting and fondue secrets.
- Franco Bordignon, of Bordignon Marble and Granite Ltd., for the marble work surface.
- Irene Waters of Hearts & Flowers Candy, Hicksville, New York, for the photo on page 41 of the Chocolate Macadamia Monet.

The authors also are indebted to Ann Merling for her wonderful food styling and to Jeff Connery of Printed Light Photography, Burnaby, B.C., for the photographs of manufacturing processes and projects in the book. Both Ann and Jeff worked incredibly hard and long hours to put together this book. Thanks to John Barrigar for his lively line drawings.

Additional photo credits: Adam's Photography, Vancouver, B.C., Canada, for the photo of Charles Sigvardsen on page 22. Kona Hilton Hotel for the photo on page 42. Sutton Place Hotel, Vancouver, B.C., for the photographs on pages 62, 63 and 64. Photos on pages 23, 77 and 78 by Shar Levine. Photo of molded chocolates on pages 12 and 13 and photo of mold on page 15, courtesy of Charlie's Chocolate Factory.

INDEX